LEADING
THE RIGHT SIDE UP

HOW TO LEAD WHEN YOU ARE NOT THE BOSS

BANKOLE AKINLADE

LEADING THE RIGHT SIDE UP

ISBN:978-0-9564767-9-1

Published by Vision Media Comm. Ltd
Email: info@colourdesigns.co.uk Tel: +44 7903 822 987

Printed in United Kingdom

What Others Are Saying About
Leading The Right Side Up

I have been involved in leading people for over 30 years. I love reading about leadership and this book has looked at many angles of leadership. This book will challenge you to lead but more importantly to serve and that is the ultimate test of leadership. **Jeffrey Lestz, CEO, Genistar Ltd.**

Leading The Right Side Up, How to lead when you are not the boss has the potential to help a wide range of leaders to appreciate they do not need to hold the lead position to be fully involved in the work of God. The tone and style of the writing make it accessible to leaders at all levels, whilst the principles outlined are practical and easy for all to apply. Bankole Akinlade has succeeded in writing a book that its readers will surely find enormously helpful. **Tope Koleoso, Lead Pastor, Jubilee Church London.**

This book is a must-read for every follower, every boss and every leader. Everyone who wishes to live in the realm of true values, walk the road called purpose and arrive at the destination called destiny must read this book. **Toheeb Dosunmu, CEO LPS Estates and QL Solutions**

I am most passionate about *'leadership'*, so what a delight it was to have read this inspiring book *Leading The Right Side Up*. This book really is a must read for all leaders and aspiring leaders. It is a Bible centred leadership tool with Christ's leadership example right at the centre! I encourage Pastors to buy a copy for all your leaders. **Peter Nembhard, Pastor, The ARC Church**

This is a fantastic book to read; a lot of thought and research has gone into this book. This book highlights themes that occur on a daily basis in politics and religion which makes it very unique and thought provoking. Once you start reading *Leading The Right Side Up* it is not easy to put the book down. I hope that everyone who reads this book finds it an interesting and easy read. **Councillor Joy Laguda MBE**

In these last days the church and our world are screaming out for gutsy, anointed leaders. Who will stand up and step forward with gritty courage to face the enormous giants of society?   This brilliant volume unpacks the principles, patterns and practices of proper Leadership. It is loaded so handle with care!!
Dr Jonathan Oloyede, Global Day of Prayer London

I consider it a great privilege to have had the pleasure of leading from behind for well over a decade. I wish I read this book earlier, I would have done a lot of things differently and perhaps commanded greater result. Leading The Right Side Up is definitely a must read for every subordinate leader, and frontline leaders who are saddled with the responsibility of mentoring them.
Godman Akinlabi, Lead Pastor, The Elevation Church Lagos.

This book is dedicated to my son,
Daniel Temiyato Akinlade,
A leader in the making.

FOREWORD

Over the last two decades or so, the teaching and theme of 'Leadership' has become quite common place in the secular and spiritual world alike. Almost every bookshop or library has a leadership section, but in my entire study life I have hardly seen a book on effective followership. I guess that is because such a book would hardly appeal to the senses of the masses. One man put it this way, that "If we all become leaders who will be the followers". I presume the more appropriate way to look at it is that no one is really ever born into a leadership position, every great leader was first an 'effective follower'.

A wise man put it this way, he said, 'The only job where you start at the top is grave digging'. I suppose he means that if you don't want to end up digging the grave of your career - start at the bottom like everybody else. In fact, as implied by the theme of this book, cultivate and maintain a 'servant's heart' even when you get to the top of the organisation.

I know no better person to write on the topic of Subordinate Leadership than Bankole Akinlade. I have known him since he walked into the church I pastor over 13 years ago and served as an employee and pastor in the same church for the last 5 years. He has always had a heart and passion to serve people in the community. He helped spearhead and oversees many of our community initiatives; he started and runs the Open House church service which reaches people of diverse backgrounds and cultures within the community.

Most importantly, Bankole has served with me in his capacity as an assistant pastor in our church leadership with a faithful, loyal and sincere heart. He loves God and God's people and as a result he has touched my heart. He evidently has the required credibility to write a book on the topic *How To Lead When You Are Not The Boss*.

Bankole has developed incredible leadership and people skills, he knows how to mobilise and galvanise people towards achieving an objective. He is a real Servant leader. Every established and aspiring leader will do well to read the book, follow the principles he teaches and as they continue to practice these things they will surely find themselves at the top of their organisation and field.

Enjoy the read.
Dr. Sola Fola-Alade
Senior Pastor, RCCG Trinity Chapel, London.

Preface

Shortly after I became a Christian, I became intrigued by the way a structure administered largely by volunteers was able to facilitate significant transformation in people's lives. And yet I could see that not all church organisations achieved the same results. On closer inspection, it seemed to me that leadership was the determining factor. Thus began my fascination with the nature of leadership. I must say even with my growing fascination, it never occurred to me that someday I might end up writing a book about leadership. My commitment to service in ministry meant that, gradually, I was given increasing responsibility for tasks and more importantly, people. I had to lead teams, through which I had to deliver set objectives. This promotion exposed my inadequacies when it came to leading people, as I soon felt that I was out of my depth. Whilst I was capable and competent at leading myself and delivering my results as long as it depended on me, doing the same through or with other people was much more demanding and at first was a source of endless frustration.

At that point I realised I needed to improve my leadership ability. I started out on a journey studying and applying the techniques for effective leadership. Thus, coupled with the changes God was working out on the inside of me, strengthened my determination to be the best leader I could be. I focused my studies especially on the life of Jesus, the greatest leader that has ever lived.

The idea of this book was first birthed when I was asked, some years back, to deliver a training session on the theme of Servant Leadership to some of our church volunteers. As I prepared for the session, its paradoxical theme crystallised in my mind the need for a book in this area. I had observed in my life as well as the lives of many others around me that leadership was desirable as long as it did not require serving others. Clearly, this was not the message that Jesus taught. He showed us that leadership is essentially servanthood and also that anyone could lead effectively without having a position or title. As I ruminated upon this idea and shared it with my pastor, Dr Sola Fola-Alade, we both agreed that it was a book worth writing; one upon which I could bring my own experiences and extensive study to bear.

Whilst writing this book, I was asked by a community organisation to speak at a 5-day leadership training session for leaders of their member organisations. I was to speak chiefly about my experience of congregational development and how the tools and skills of community organising could be used effectively in faith-based institutions. . At the end of my brief talk, I agreed to answer a few questions. The first question was from a lady representing her South London-based church. She asked, 'As I am not the senior leader in my organisation, how can I be expected to influence others to follow me in order to achieve an agreed course of action?' As I had already started writing this book, I took the opportunity to gauge interest in the theme of my book. I briefly shared snippets from this book with those in attendance.

At the end of the presentation, a significant number of those in attendance were keen to get their hands on a copy of the book. Evidently, the snippets from the book which I shared and discussed during the session proved popular with the audience and I was further encouraged to complete the book.

The question the lady from south London asked is one I have grappled with for many years, and I am sure that many sub-tier leaders in other organisations can relate to it too. The fact of the matter is that most people will not get the opportunity to lead from the number one spot, and it is with this reality in mind that this book has been written. I want to map a path to leadership for those who do not necessarily hold a position or title within their organisations.

The principles shared in this book will raise your leadership bar and help you lead courageously and confidently from wherever you are within your organisation.

ACKNOWLEDGEMENTS

This work was made possible by God. 2011 was a year packed with the most commitments in my life to date; it has been indeed a year of divine assistance.

My wife, Funmi has been incredible and very accommodating of the demands I placed on myself. Even when we were on our holidays, I continued to write. I also appreciate the fact that you were on hand to help as my first-line editor and also through the next few editing stages of the book. I am eternally grateful. I remain yours forever.

Eunice Awosika's effort in transcribing my initial audio teaching served as the much needed canvas upon which I started to write this book earlier in 2011. Thanks. Ade Adewunmi, my critic and second-line editor was central to the completion of this work. With the skill you brought to editing this book, I wondered if you are in the right profession. You've helped greatly, and I deeply appreciate your contributions. Thanks also to my friend, Jinmi Macaulay for all the late nights spent working on my manuscript.

I especially want to thank Dr Sola Fola-Alade, a true leader whose life and ministry has greatly impacted my life. He challenged me to pursue this dream and encouraged me throughout the writing. Whilst some people have different people who play the role of boss, mentor and pastor in their life, I consider myself privileged to have all three rolled up in one person, Dr Fola-Alade. His quest for knowledge and his heart for people continue to challenge me.

Serving at Trinity Chapel has given me a wonderful opportunity to meet many great people whom I serve alongside, both staff and laity. I am indebted to you all who have in many ways have helped improve my leadership. It has been a pleasure serving you.

CONTENTS

INTRODUCTION

'Pharaoh also said to Joseph, "I am Pharaoh, and without your consent no man may lift his hand or foot in all the land of Egypt.' – Genesis 41: 44

'You don't have to hold a position in order to be a leader.' – Anthony J D'Angelo

I n the summer of 2009, my wife and I, together with a younger cousin of mine and a couple of other friends, went on a road trip to Paris for a few days. It was the first time we had all travelled together. It was also the first time our car had been taken on such a trip. As a result, I took sole responsibility for the long drive from London to Paris.

My cousin, who at the time had only recently acquired his driver's licence, offered to drive, but I did not take him up on the offer. I was uncomfortable with relinquishing the responsibility for our collective well-being to him. The thing was, while he was licensed to drive and had some driving experience under his belt, I had not tested him, nor could I be certain that he had *enough* experience to get us safely to our destination. Further, I found his eagerness to drive somewhat worrying, as it did not seem to me at the time that he had paid due consideration to the weight of the task. Although we were both able to drive, I felt we were driven by different agendas. I felt I was more concerned with the safety of the vehicle and passengers as we journeyed through uncharted territories. Meanwhile, I got the sense that for my cousin, his overriding interest was the thrill of the experience – a badge of honour of his driving acumen, something he could boast about to his friends.

To some degree, that trip to Paris illustrates the essence of leading, as the goal was to move people towards an agreed destination. It also depicts an oft-familiar relationship: the one between the person ultimately responsible and the other(s) who is similarly interested in taking on the responsibility for (in this case, literally) driving others to a given destination. Wherever there are two or more people with a common goal, the opportunity arises for one person to take responsibility. Thus, one person, either by appointment or by assumption, steps into this role. In organisations, the one playing this leadership role in a group of two or more people is colloquially known as 'the boss'. Bosses come in different forms, but they all play a significant role within their organisations and, particularly, in the lives of those who report directly to them. The position of 'the boss' is an enviable one and many people aspire to it, if only for the extra benefits it commands, rather than its accompanying responsibilities. So, what makes the boss 'The Boss'? I would argue it's the fact that he or she is ultimately responsible for ensuring the success of their organisation.

THE SUBORDINATE LEADER

The object of this book, however, is not the role or responsibilities of the boss, but has as its focus the leader who leads from within any organisation. The scenario given earlier highlights the often common desire amongst subordinates to trade in their role as assistants for the leading role. The truth of the matter is that you do not have to be in the driver's seat to play an equally important leadership role. My cousin had an equally, if not a more important, role to play on our trip in that I received directions from him because he was responsible for interpreting the directions on the map we had with us to ensure that we arrived safely at our destination. Without this role, our trip could have been a disaster. The role played by subordinate leaders is very significant to the success of all organisations, but many do not know it.

Do You Have a Boss at the Helm or a Leader?

Theodore Roosevelt, the former American president, once said, 'People ask the difference between a leader and a boss. The leader leads, and the boss drives.' The boss drives people within organisations to achieve desired success, while leaders inspire and influence people along in order to achieve success together. A leader is a person whose life and actions inspire and influence others to achieve a common goal together. When bosses achieve results, the people say, 'He did it,' but when a leader achieves results, the people say, 'We did it.' There are bosses that are leaders and there are many leaders that are not bosses.

JESUS, THE GREATEST LEADER THAT EVER LIVED

Being a boss is not the same thing as being a leader. Holding the position of 'boss' does not make one a leader. As a boss, you can hit all your targets, whilst not necessarily having *led* the people. So, if being the boss is not the same thing as leading, then what does it mean to lead? In the New Testament, Jesus Christ, the greatest leader that ever walked the face of the earth, taught a model of leadership, which showed that it is possible to lead without having the position or title of 'boss'. He was neither a king nor a governor, yet even today, many are still influenced by his life and model of leadership. Concerning Jesus, General Napoleon Bonaparte remarked, 'Alexander, Caesar, Charlemagne, and myself founded empires, but what foundation did we rest the creations of our genius? Upon force. Jesus Christ founded an empire upon love, and at this hour millions of men would die for Him.'

It took me several years to begin to grasp what Jesus taught about leadership, and as I finally began to grasp His concept of leadership, I became convinced that anyone can lead, even without a title or official position. His model of leadership turns the common notion of leadership on its head, and the truly great leaders in history have shown that Jesus had it the right side up.

Martin Luther King said, 'Everybody can be great because anybody can serve. You don't have to have a college degree to serve. You don't have to make your subject and verb agree to serve. You only need a heart full of grace. A soul generated by love.' The ability to get a hold of this truth means that everyone can lead, regardless of their official title or position within an organisation. So, whether from the position of chief executive officer or a cleaner, or as a pastor or a parishioner, leadership is possible. Leading is more than merely completing the task at hand, whether great or small. Leaders know that beyond the task lies what leaders do best, which is to influence people.

NO ROOM FOR EVERYONE AT THE TOP

There is a commonly used expression: 'See you at the top.' This sounds great and encouraging, but it is hardly feasible in practice. After all, if everyone aimed for and succeeded in getting to the top spot, it wouldn't be the 'top' anymore. It would be the new bottom floor. However, the reality that, by definition, not everyone can make it to the 'top' is a fact of life that many aspiring leaders don't like to consider. Understandably so – after all, the bottom is crowded. Unfortunately, however unpalatable, the truth is that there will never be enough room at the top for everyone. Furthermore, anyone who is waiting to get to the top before beginning to influence others is unlikely to ever get there. The key, therefore, is to begin to lead from wherever you are. As John Maxwell rightly noted, 99 percent of all leadership occurs not from the top but from the middle of the organisation.[1]

At times, as Christians, we feel like we are not 'fully in God's will' except when we are leading from the top. In truth, though, a leader's rise (or not) to the top spot isn't necessarily an indication of God's activity in his or her life. In fact, one could get to the very top and find out that you have pursued your own ambitions for your life rather than God's agenda.

No other example in the Bible better illustrates this point than the life of Joseph as recorded in Genesis chapters 37, 39-45. Joseph came from a privileged background and had lofty dreams and aspirations. Though his dreams were eventually actualised, it did not happen in the way Joseph had expected. There are five key lessons we can learn from Joseph's life, namely:

1. Joseph had dreams and aspirations – Dreams and aspirations are the stuff leaders are made of. Every leader has aspirations for a better future and so did Joseph. He dreamt of leading his clan and he made no apologies for his dreams because he was convinced that they were God's plans for his life. What he was less certain of was: how he would realise his dream and how long it would take to be realised. Nothing prepared him for the many years of challenges to follow.

2. Joseph feared God and was conscious of God's presence – With the benefit of hindsight, we see that God was with Joseph all through his life's journey, up to and beyond his promotion to the palace. Joseph must have believed that God was nearby and watching his every move. This awareness of God's presence is discernable in his response to Potiphar's wife as he resisted her sexual advances (as recorded in Genesis 39). His reaction also demonstrated a healthy fear of offending God.

3. Joseph learnt humility and developed character through his suffering – Many times, God uses challenges to improve our character. It was evident that when Joseph had the dreams, he was quite young and whilst internalizing the dreams, pride set in, and so affected his relationship with his siblings and his father. The pit and prison experiences helped build character in him.

4. Joseph was always on hand to help others – At a time when he was wrestling with his own issues, Joseph still found the time to listen to others and to help them

through their own challenges. He was known as a problem solver and the go to person. These inherent attributes recommended him for positions of leadership. For example, after being sold to Potiphar as a slave, he quickly rose to become the overseer of Potiphar's estate. Similarly, following his wrongful imprisonment on allegations of sexual abuse, he was given charge over all the prisoners. In spite of the fact that his prospects for achieving any of his own dreams appeared bleak, he still found it in his heart to interpret the dreams of Pharaoh's servants (as recorded in Genesis 40). It was this act that got him a recommendation to Pharaoh when the latter had a dream that stumped his team of counsellors.

5. He influenced those around him – Joseph understood the power and importance of influence. He influenced Potiphar (Genesis 39:3), the prison guards (Genesis 40:4) and his fellow prisoners (Genesis 40:7-23). He even influenced Pharaoh the king himself (Genesis 41), and as a result, went on to exert influence throughout Egypt (Genesis 41:44).

Just as importantly though, Joseph's influence wasn't limited to the public sphere. Reading through the scriptures, we see that he also had influence within his own family. Joseph wasn't the head of his family or the nation of Egypt and yet he had influence. This is because at its core, leadership has a lot to do with influencing people for good. Consequently, Joseph was able to lead without holding the 'number one' position. Influence is really a matter of disposition rather than

Influence is really a matter of disposition rather than position.

position. Joseph developed the disposition of a leader and so became a leader who made his journey from the pit, through the prisons and into the palace.

THE LEADING FOLLOWER

Great leaders are first great followers. **Great leaders** Prior to Joshua exercising great **are first great** leadership, we read in the biblical **followers.** scriptures of how he first faithfully served as an assistant to Moses. Many leaders have followed a very similar trajectory. God usually observes one's faithfulness in much lesser assignments before commissioning one to lead. Often times, subordinate leaders are impatient to take charge. Such impatience, in many respects, shows the limitations of the subordinate's character development.

When Dwight Eisenhower served as the president of the United States, Richard Nixon served alongside him as his vice president. It was said that though President Eisenhower had a high regard for Nixon's skill and intelligence, he was concerned with the latter's seemingly awkward disposition as a leader, and his failure to grow in character.[2] Nixon went on to become president of the United States in 1968. However, while he obviously had the charisma and the will to achieve his goal of becoming president, he lacked the character to uphold the office. The Watergate scandal, which led to his resignation, clearly exposed character flaws that he had failed to work on during his days of obscurity as an aspiring leader.

Andy Stanley, Pastor of North Point Community Church in Atlanta, Georgia, USA, made an interesting observation about subordinate leaders. He noted that when a leader is leading other leaders, there is usually a feeling amongst the subordinate leaders that they could do a better job than the leader.[3] The Bible bears witness to these tendencies amongst subordinate leaders as recorded in the case of Aaron and Miriam in Numbers 12. Both Miriam and Aaron felt that they had a higher moral ground on which to challenge Moses, God's chosen leader. Even if they had been correct in their analyses, their wrong disposition, as revealed by their statements, 'Has the Lord indeed only spoken through Moses? Has He not spoken through us also?' (Numbers 12:2) showed them to be unworthy. And we see that God dealt with them accordingly. Unlike Joshua, they disqualified themselves from being next in line for leadership. It bears noting that Aaron started out as Moses' assistant, but somewhere along the lines, he lost his place to Joshua.

Moses could not have been the easiest leader to assist with his anger-management issues and other evident flaws, yet Joshua served him diligently. Similarly, Eisenhower himself served in many capacities as a subordinate leader. He was said to have served under General Douglas MacArthur and General George Marshall, who were the most notable generals of his day. His exemplary service to other leaders earned him a place as one of America's most popular presidents.[4]

Leadership is learnt in the trenches, not on the throne, and so the right time to learn how to lead is now – right where you are. In this book, I will outline how to lead from

Leadership is learnt in the trenches, not on the throne

whatever position you are in within your organisation – in other words, when you're *not* the boss! As you read this book, it will shape your understanding of Christian leadership and equip you to lead by showing you how to build influence within your organisation, and as a result, make you an asset to your organisation.

CHAPTER ONE

THE CALL TO LEAD

'To aspire to leadership is an honourable ambition.'
– 1 Timothy 3:1 (NEB)

'Anyone can lead, but not everyone is called to
leadership.' – Bankole Akinlade

The words 'leader' and 'leadership' only really became part of my functional vocabulary when I joined my current church, several years ago. Prior to that, I had never considered myself a leader, nor even imagined that I would become one. Nonetheless, the church's mission statement, which is 'Developing Leaders, Influencing Society' struck a chord deep within me. I knew I wanted to be a part of it. This was in spite of the fact that, at the time, my perspective on leadership was hazy.

It took several years of hearing the church's mission statement reinforced in many Sunday sermons, attending church conferences with gurus such as John Maxwell and Myles Monroe, reading their books and others', before the concept of leadership sunk in. I suspect that my journey was not a unique one. I imagine that for others just like me, words such as leading, leader and leadership conjure up different things for different people. I also imagine that such thoughts on leaders and leadership have been shaped by our experiences and influenced by views of men and women we respect, either in books or other media. Broadly speaking, people react to the concept of leadership in four ways, and these reactions are shaped by their perspectives. People react with:

- Desire – A few months back, I asked two young people to attend a leadership meeting in my stead. In passing on the invite, I mentioned that one of the reasons why I had asked them to represent me was that I considered them to be leaders. I later learnt, rather amusingly, that one of them was over the moon at the thought of being referred to as a leader. So much so, that he mentioned this to anyone around him who cared to listen. He really liked the idea of being thought of as a leader. This was in spite of the fact that he would have struggled to articulate what leadership really entailed.

- Disinterest – To someone drawn to leadership, it's hard to comprehend why people, particularly those who have a leadership gift, sit on the sidelines and refuse to take on the responsibility of leading. There is nothing wrong in taking a back seat sometimes and allowing others to lead; however, in my experience, that isn't the main reason for this attitude. Rather, I've observed that many of those who are indifferent to leadership opportunities do so because they do not want to take responsibility. In particular, they don't want to be held responsible if things go wrong.

- Despise – This reaction is understandable when we consider the abuse of office by leaders on the global scale. Leaders of nations who commit atrocities against their own people or plunder their nations' resources fall into this category. So do leaders of multinational corporations or churches tasked with serving their staff and customers or congregations respectively, who take advantage of their leadership role to enrich themselves or exploit the vulnerable. If these people are truly representative of the essence of leadership, then disgust and loathing are not unreasonable sentiments. Many who react to the idea of leadership with these types of negative emotions have often been direct or indirect victims of abuses of leadership. Consequently, they look upon leaders with disdain and mistrust.

- A Sense of Duty – Some people have been conditioned from a young age to 'step up' and take responsibility. Such people tend to be innate leaders who have stepped into leadership at a young age. Such people cannot just sit back and watch things go wrong or go undone. It is simply who they are. In part, they might even be oblivious of the technical term of what they are doing. A biblical example is Moses. Moses' sense of duty to his people meant that he simply couldn't walk away when he saw a fellow Israelite being ill-treated by an Egyptian. Similarly, he felt compelled to intervene when he saw two Israelites quarrelling. His interventions weren't well implemented (or particularly appreciated), but we can clearly see that he was motivated by a sense of responsibility or duty, even though he had no official leadership role.

DEFINITION OF LEADERSHIP
Leadership has been defined in many different ways, and there is no universally accepted definition of leadership. Rather, each definition seeks to contribute something new to the many other definitions. So, instead of crafting yet another definition, I have outlined a few of the ones I consider most helpful.

Some Definitions of Leadership
1. Leadership is influence – J. Oswald Sanders
2. Leadership is getting others to want to do something that you are convinced should be done – Vance Packard
3. Leadership is doing the right things – Warren Bennis and Burt Nanus
4. Leadership is the ability to get other people to do what they don't want to do and like it – Harry Truman
5. Leadership is a dynamic process in which a man or woman with God-given capacity influences a specific group of God's people toward His purposes for the group – Dr. Robert Clinton

While these are all good and true definitions of leadership, for our purposes, I believe the definitions offered by James Hunter[1] and Henry and Richard Blackaby[2] will serve us best.

In his book, *The World's Most Powerful Leadership Principle*, James Hunter gives a comprehensive definition of leadership as, 'The skills of influencing people to enthusiastically work toward goals identified as being for the common good, with character that inspires confidence.'

Hunter's definition does well in capturing the essence of leadership in a single statement. Henry and Richard Blackaby, in their book, *Spiritual Leadership*, also give a concise definition of leadership for the Christian leader. They define spiritual leadership as, 'Moving people on to God's agenda.'

These two definitions encapsulate the ideas that I will attempt to deconstruct in the rest of this book.

WHAT LEADERSHIP IS NOT

Just as we can seek to define what leadership is, we can also be clear about what leadership is not. Such knowledge will also play a role in shaping our understanding of leadership. Leadership is *not*:

1. Manipulating people – To manipulate means to persuade others for the sole purpose of personal benefit. This goes against the grain of what leadership is about, which is seeking to influence people for mutual benefit. True leadership is found in giving oneself in service alongside others, not in coaxing or inducing others to serve.
2. Merely directing people – Leaders don't just point the way. They 'go the way' *and* take others with them. A quote from the commentary in the John Maxwell Study Bible articulates this most aptly. It reads, 'the more leaders walk, the less they need to talk.'
3. Charisma – As a leader, having charisma is great, but it does not by itself make a leader. Leadership is not

synonymous with charisma. Being charismatic is a gift and though it does help, the lack of it does not diminish a leader. Peter Drucker, the management guru, is quoted as saying, 'leadership is not popularity; it's about results.'[3] Charisma may cause people to take interest, but it will not cause them to follow.

4. Necessarily management – For quite some time, I equated leadership with management. I now know it is possible to be a good manager and yet be poor at leading. Management has to do with engaging the mind and the hands as a resource in order to achieve a desired goal. Leadership precedes that by first seeking to engage the heart.

IS EVERYONE CALLED TO LEADERSHIP?

When Jesus called Andrew and Peter his brother to follow Him, as recorded in Matthew 4:19, little did they know it would result in their playing a leading role in history. The call to lead often starts as a call to follow. From a Christian point of view, God first calls people to follow Him before he puts them on the path to leadership.

The call to lead often starts as a call to follow.

Earlier this year, while delivering a series of lessons on leadership to a team that I lead, I was asked an age-old question by one of them. It is a question which most people have asked when contemplating the nature of leadership. She asked, "Is everyone called to be a leader?" It is a question that I grappled with for many years, too.

Matthew 20:20-22 reads:

'Then the mother of Zebedee's sons came to Him with her sons, kneeling down and asking something from Him. And He said to her, "What do you wish?" She said to Him, "Grant that these two sons of mine may sit, one on Your right hand and the other on the left, in Your Kingdom."

'But Jesus answered and said, "You do not know what you ask. Are you able to drink the cup that I am about to drink, and be baptized with the baptism that I am baptized with?" They said to Him, "We are able." So He said to them, "You will indeed drink My cup, and be baptized with the baptism that I am baptized with; but to sit on My right hand and on My left is not Mine to give, but it is for those whom it is prepared by My father.'

In this scripture, we see the mother of the Zebedee brothers come before Jesus, probably after having a private conversation with her sons (James and John) with a request. Her request is that her two sons be given positions of authority (the seats to the right and left of Jesus) in Jesus' kingdom. Her motivation was a desire to secure positions of honour for her sons in Jesus' kingdom. Her ideas about leadership and position are very similar to those of many of us today. On the back of that event, Jesus taught two very important lessons:

1. The cost associated with leadership: Jesus asked them, 'Are you able to drink the cup that I am about to drink, and be baptized with the baptism that I am baptized with?' What He was really pointing out was that becoming the type of leader worthy of occupying such lofty positions would come at a great cost.

2. God calls specific types of people to certain positions of leadership: Jesus said to them, 'but to sit on My right hand and on My left is not Mine to give, but it is for those whom it is prepared by My father.' According to God's divine plan, each one has a place where they best fit. He prepares the place for us and also prepares us for the place. Through a series of events in our lives, we are then guided to that place.

Generally, every Christian is called to be light in the world (Matthew 5:14), and more specifically, each of us is called to a definite purpose (1 Corinthians 12:28), and so in calling us, it is His expectation that we have a measure of influence with people in whatever we are called to. If God expects us to have influence, then in that sense, we are all called to lead.

GOD'S TRI-FOCAL CALLING

When Christians speak of God's calling, we often assume it has to do with full-time church ministry. I know of people that are doing phenomenal work as business leaders, project managers, sports personalities and more – all of whom are called by God to serve in those capacities. There are three dimensions to God's calling, and it is only as we yield in these dimensions that we are truly able to lead.

•   **Firstly, God calls us to a walk with Him**. This is the primary call of every believer. It's a walk in fellowship with God and is the life source of every Christian leader. Apostle Paul said, 'Pattern yourselves after me [follow my example], as I imitate and follow Christ [the messiah]' – 1 Corinthians 11:1 (amplified version). No Christian leader should lead if he or she is not first following Christ.

- **Secondly, God calls us to work for Him.** Every believer is called to some work. In our work, God expects us to represent Him and to project the values of the kingdom. Whether as a sportsman, a scientist or a school teacher, we are ambassadors of Christ. We may not all be called to the five-fold ministry, but we are all ministers, whether in the marketplace or ministry. Though you might argue that you go to work for an employer and they pay your wages, nevertheless, you work for God and you ought to do the work at an outstanding level of excellence unto God.

- **Thirdly, God calls us to a walk with others.** Our walk with God is impacted by our walk with others. As God's ambassadors, the examples we set in the way that we relate with and serve others should cause people to follow Christ. 'Let your light so shine before men, that they may see your good works and glorify your Father in heaven' – Matthew 5:16.

ARE LEADERS BORN OR ARE LEADERS MADE?

There is a never-ending debate about this question with no consensus in sight. Aristotle, the Greek philosopher, is believed to have said, 'Some men are born to lead and others to be led.[4] Others disagree with this line of thinking, and in their book, *Called to be God's Leader*, Henry and Richard Blackaby categorically state that there is no such thing as a born leader.[5] John Maxwell takes a more lighthearted view in seeking consensus on the view that all leaders are born. He goes on to state that from this starting point, every other important aspect of leadership can be learnt. In other words, leaders can also be made.[6] In responding to the same question, Peter

Drucker is alleged to have said that while there might be 'born leaders', it makes little difference in the grand scheme of things, as they are few and far between.[7]

Personally, I take the view that, whilst it is true that some people possess a greater proportion of the natural attributes often associated with leadership, the skills required to lead effectively still have to be developed.

Jeremiah – Called to Lead as a Prophet
God calls people to particular tasks, equips them for that role, and helps them grow into the role. We learn that this was the experience of young Jeremiah, as recorded in Jeremiah 1:5;

'Before I formed you in the womb I knew you; before you were born I sanctified you; I ordained [called] you a prophet to the nations.'

Before Jeremiah was born, God had ordained him to fulfil a specific role as a prophet to the nations. His call also meant that he was 'wired' to fulfil that role, and that meant being able to see and hear God clearly. Jeremiah however, had to develop into that role, and so we see a part of the growth process in verses 11-12 of Jeremiah 1; *'Moreover the word of the Lord came to me, saying, "Jeremiah, what do you see?" And I said, "I see a branch of an almond tree. " Then the Lord said to me, "You have seen well, for I am ready to perform my word."'*

While some of the great leaders in the Bible were shown to have been called from birth to do something great and worthy of mention in scriptures, for others like David, it was not so. David became God's chosen leader because

God saw David's faithfulness and commitment while tending his father's sheep. It was these characteristics that caused God to raise him up as a king over His people in Israel.

God calls people to lead in different capacities and spheres and we are all able to lead if we learn to imbibe the attributes that leaders possess, which are outlined in subsequent chapters. Each one of us is given an opportunity to lead and that begins with leading oneself – a responsibility, which is always more difficult to achieve than leading others.

THE CALL TO LEADERSHIP

The Bible is littered with examples of people with talents in the areas of pastoral, hospitality and evangelistic ministries *as well as* the spiritual gift of leadership.

'Here are some of the parts God has appointed for the church: first are apostles, second are prophets, third are teachers, then those who do miracles, those who have the gift of healing, those who can help others, those who have the gift of leadership, those who speak in unknown languages.' – *1 Corinthians 12:28 (NLT)*

Those gifted in this way are equipped to become great leaders and are also able to teach others to lead effectively. In his book, *Leaders on Leadership*, George Barna defined eight key signs that indicate that a person has been called by God to lead.[8] These eight signs are:

- Sensing the call
- Undeniable inclination
- Mind of a leader

- Discernible influence
- The company of leaders
- External encouragement
- Internal strength
- Loving it

Let's explore these eight indicators or signs in greater detail:

- Sensing the call: George Barna asserts that those that have been called by God to lead have a sense or knowing that God has, indeed, called them to be significant in their society by leading others to Him. Whilst such people may not immediately obey the call, evidence provided by the Holy Spirit continues to verify or reaffirm the call until it is undeniable to them.

- Undeniable inclination: Leaders generally feel an urge or inclination to lead. The leader may either be thrust into a position of leadership as a result of unique or unusual events or circumstances, as was the case for Timothy and Nehemiah, or be drawn to take up a leadership role due to a natural enthusiasm.

- Mind of a leader: This indicator is concerned with a distinctive perspective that leaders tend to adopt. They tend to focus on the vision of the organisation and think about the long-term implications of current choices. As a result, leaders tend to be strategic thinkers, often focusing on the big picture and not so much on the fine detail.

- Discernible influence: This refers to the evidence of a direct impact of a leader in the lives of those he or she has been called, by God, to lead. There will be tangible examples of people's lives being changed for the better following their interaction with such leaders.

- The company of leaders: In other words, birds of a feather flock together. People are drawn to people who they have things in common with. It's no different with leaders. God-called leaders tend to be drawn to like-minded people – that is, leaders will tend to be surrounded by other leaders.

- External encouragement: Leadership characteristics tend to attract notice. Consequently, people with leadership qualities tend to be noticed or affirmed by others. The affirmation of this special capability is of most value when it comes from other true leaders.

- Internal strength. Leadership requires one to quite literally 'take the lead' and this is often an exercise fraught with uncertainty. It requires leaders to be comfortable taking reasonable risks and traversing unchartered territory. Those called to lead have the inner courage to stand by their decisions regardless of the consequences. Jesus is a key example of this.

- Loving it. Even though God's leaders face controversy and confrontation, they understand that regardless of these obstacles, accomplishing the vision is worth it all.

When God calls a leader in this way, it soon becomes evident to all around. **God uses** Over time, the distinctiveness in the **experiences to** person's life that sets him/her apart **shape leaders**.

begins to manifest as they gracefully exercise leadership and also teach others to do the same.

GOD'S LEADERSHIP PREP SCHOOL

In addition to being gifted to lead, God uses experiences to shape leaders. By this I mean He orchestrates events in a person's life that prepares them for leadership. These events are usually a combination of life experiences as outlined below.

THE POWER OF ADVERSITY

When contemplating life as a leader, it is easier and more palatable to envision a future with many people at one's beck and call rather than to see oneself in a position of service. This was Joseph's experience. Here was a young boy who in a dream saw his parents and siblings bowing down to him. Barely able to contain his excitement, he tactlessly shared this dream with those directly impacted by it.

Joseph started out with a strong desire to lead, but as demonstrated by his careless disregard for the feelings of others, he was not yet ready to lead. Instead, God used a series of challenges to develop his character and to mould him into a true leader. Joseph's many adversities were God's training sessions. He used them to weave into Joseph's life the essence of a true leader. I will expand on this further in subsequent chapters. Suffice it to say that by the time Joseph appeared before Pharaoh, his character had been tempered – so much so that it quickly became evident to Pharaoh and his advisers that Joseph was the man to solve the crisis that was looming over the nation of Egypt. God had prepared him for such a challenge.

The entire Israelite community in Egypt enjoyed much prosperity and freedom for many centuries as a direct result of Joseph's service to Egypt. In other words, his efforts had indirectly paved the way for them to succeed. With the benefit of hindsight, Joseph could see that though his brothers had intended his destruction by selling him into slavery, God had turned that awful experience around for his benefit, and ultimately for the benefit of the wider Israelite community.

Similarly, Abraham Lincoln's many failures are well documented. He suffered two failed attempts at marriage, a failed business in a booming economy, and failure in his first foray into politics. Through all those failures, he learnt a key lesson that he summed up, 'Without divine assistance, I cannot succeed; with it, I cannot fail.'

What lesson can we take from the experiences of Joseph and Abraham Lincoln in the 'school' of adversity? Adversity does not disqualify anyone from being a leader; rather, it should be seen as one of the tools through which God embeds certain leadership qualities that are vital for effective leadership.

DIVINE ENCOUNTERS
Another way God moulds His leaders is through encounters that leave indelible marks upon their lives. Such encounters become a cornerstone in a leader's development. Apostle Paul's ambition was to eradicate the followers of Christ. He was willing to spend his life ensuring that he fulfilled that ambition. Whilst on one of his self-appointed crusades, he had a divine encounter – a vision of Christ that changed his life's mission. That

experience turned a self-appointed destroyer of Christ's mission into a self-acclaimed 'servant of Christ', a true leader of the faith. The impact of encountering Christ caused Paul to later regard his various worldly accolades and accomplishments (as a learned Jew, schooled under the tutelage of the erudite Jewish scholar, Gamaliel) as loss when compared with knowing Christ. His encounter etched an indelible mark upon his life forever. For what Paul was called to do, such an unforgettable experience served as fuel that kept his passion for God alive to the very end.

MOTIVATED BY A CAUSE

All David wanted to do was to shepherd his father's sheep, and this he did passionately even to the point of endangering his own life by fighting off and killing wild animals that threatened the sheep.

While carrying out the mundane business of tending his father's sheep, external events conspired to cause his life to take a markedly different turn. During a food delivery errand to the battlefield, he happened to witness a soldier from the Philistine army taunt his national army and blaspheme his God. The fact that his cowed national army could only look on in humiliated silence was too much for David to bear. Motivated by the cause of defending his national honour, he challenged Goliath to a duel. His act of extreme bravery delivered God's people (1 Samuel 17:29).

The late Mother Teresa of Calcutta is known worldwide for her work with the poor people in India. Though she enjoyed her missionary work as a teacher in Calcutta, she was gripped by the poverty around her, which led to the launch of the Missionaries of Charity, set up to help the poorest among the poor. On the surface, these two examples seem to be polar opposites. However, look a little more closely and you'll see that in both cases, gripped by a cause, ordinary people overcame seemingly insurmountable obstacles. That's the power of a cause. What's yours?

EDUCATION

Often times when we think of the ways God prepares people for leadership, we don't consider education. However, it is one the ways He prepares people for positions of leadership. It is believed that Moses was educated in the best schools of Egypt at the time and raised under the tutelage of Pharaoh, the king of Egypt (Acts 7:22). This schooling in the customs and beliefs of Egyptian high society prepared Moses for the great task of engaging with Pharaoh and leading God's people out of slavery. Education provides leaders with the mental aptitude required to analyse situations and challenges and to proffer best solutions.

The Redeemed Christian Church of God's General overseer, Pastor E. A. Adeboye, has a PHD in mathematics. His educational heights attracted many other well-educated people to the denomination, which was previously founded by an illiterate. God also used his educational exposure and that of his pastors to take this ministry, which was initially domiciled in Nigeria, to become a global phenomenon with more than 20,000 church parishes located in 140 nations of the world.

Bishop Desmond Tutu, a Nobel Peace Prize winner, once claimed that he became a 'leader by default, only because nature does not allow a vacuum.' Looking into his background, his education at Kings College London, one of the best universities in the UK, in the 1960s prepared him to take a leading role in the reconciliation process after South Africa's apartheid regime. While it might appear to the casual observer that, as Reverend Tutu self-effacingly says, he became a 'leader by default', I would argue that God worked through his education and the knowledge he acquired through it.

And whilst the examples I have cited highlight the impact of education, it is important to note that education does not always have to be structured or classroom based.

When it comes to shaping leaders, with God everything counts. However, He doesn't tend to act unilaterally when raising leaders, and so the way we respond to our opportunities and experiences determine whether we realise our leadership potential or not.

WHO WILL GO FOR US?
'Then I heard the voice of the Lord saying, "Whom shall I send? And who will go for us?"' – Isaiah 6:8 (NIV)

It is quite intriguing that God would put such a query to anyone. Surely, He must have known that someone would take on the assignment. Yet I cannot but wonder what would have happened if the prophet Isaiah didn't respond to that call. Personally, I find it a little unsettling that God might rely on the willingness of people to respond to His call (which often appears as an apparent need in society). I would find it more reassuring for God to call a person outright and make His call evident to such.

A very inspiring scripture that further elucidates this point is found in 2 Corinthians 8:16-17, in which Apostle Paul talks about Titus, a young leader and protégé of his.

'But thanks be to God who puts the same earnest care for you into the heart of Titus. For he not only accepted the exhortation, but being more diligent, he went to you of his own accord.'

During a sermon preached in January of 2008, Pastor Sola Fola-Alade of Trinity Chapel in London spoke of his heart's desire for the rehabilitation of the drug addicts who regularly loiter in Camden town in North London. When Henry Akuffo heard Pastor Sola's words, he was moved to respond to the situation. This led to the creation of the Freedom Project, an initiative set up in partnership with Teen Challenge and volunteers from other churches in the community to meet the needs of addicts within the London borough of Newham.

One of the key qualities of leadership is being able to take the initiative to act. And it seems that God makes opportunities available, seeking those who will respond by taking the initiative. Henry, who had battled addiction in the past, had developed a passion for the rehabilitation of drug and alcohol addicts. In time, after many years of preparation, he was able to respond to God's call, which came in the form of a message from the pulpit. It has by no means been a challenge-free or convenient experience for him, but seeing the lives transformed has certainly made it a worthwhile and fulfilling one.

God still calls out today expecting that we will volunteer ourselves in response to His need. In doing so, many have found the sphere in which they have been called to influence: to lead.

CHAPTER TWO

THE CORE OF LEADERSHIP

'And he answered, "You shall love the Lord your God with all your heart and with all your soul and with all your strength and with all your mind, and your neighbor as yourself."' Luke 10:27 (ESV)

'Good leaders make people feel that they're at the very heart of things, not at the periphery.'
- Warren G. Bennis

The scriptures record a number of times that Jesus was often asked what the most essential law or principle of the Kingdom of God was. In response to such queries, Christ outlined the true basis for Christian living, which is:

1. Love God.
2. Love your neighbour.

These two elements form the crux of all that Christian life is about and, so, should shape the Christian leader's view of leadership.

THE BOTTOM LINE

In business, the 'bottom line' is the deciding or crucial factor in decision making. It is what matters most to the stakeholders in the business; it's the core and the essential reason why the organisation exists. Extending the commercial analogy to leadership, what is the 'bottom line' of leadership? What gets **Following** the leader out of bed in the morning and **Christ,** shapes his or her thoughts and decisions? **Serving** For the Christian leader, that 'bottom line' **People** can be articulated in a single phrase, 'Following Christ, Serving People.'

This bottom line does not apply only to leadership in a church or ministry setting, but rather should form the basis for engagement in all areas of life. It is always inspiring to hear stories of Christian business leaders who are building businesses that are changing people's lives and are based on Christian principles. Recently, I met a lady whose life was transformed when she started to work with Genistar, a financial education company co-owned and led by Jeffrey Lestz. Despite her atheist background and her personal views on religion, the love of God reached her as a result of her interaction with this business and broke into her life in an amazing way. Genistar's business, started in 2007, is FSA regulated and through its 3,000 associates, who have been trained using biblical principles,[1] has empowered more than 7,000 people to achieve their financial goals. There are many successful businesses and organisations that hold people and Godly principles at the core of what they do. Of course, there are many other organisations that do not hold these fundamental values, yet still experience extraordinary success. However, from a Christian point of view, leadership in any field warrants that Godly principles underscore the decisions and shape the actions of the leaders.

In his book, *Anointed for Business*,[2] Ed Silvoso wrote about an employee of the Argentinean prison system who had a vision of becoming a prison warden. His vision became a reality when he was asked, less than five years later, to become the warden of a large prison in Argentina. Being a Christian, he set out to establish Godly principles amongst the guards and inmates. As a result, that particular prison became one of the best run in Argentina. As a warden, he had limited control because he still had bosses to report to, but his conviction to have God at the centre of his work led him to deduce and apply biblical principles in the running of the prison. The outcome was a transformed prison and an improvement in the lives of the inmates in that prison.

Jesus came to show us that our relationship with God and people are the two most important things in life. The success of His ministry can be traced back to his essential relationship with God the Father. Everything He did in the lives of people was as a result of what He saw the Father do. What set Him apart as a leader was His relationship with God and His desire for meaningful relationships and impact in the lives of those He interacted with.

CHRIST-CENTRED LEADERSHIP

I never cease to be amazed by people who express interest in leading, yet who do not seek to submit to any authority in their own lives. Recently, during a leadership programme I organised, I asked the delegates to demonstrate their agreement with the ethos of the programme by signing a document to that effect. I did this because I wanted them to be clear about what the training would involve and to ascertain their commitment. The first commitment I requested from them was that they 'agree to surrender completely to the leadership of Jesus Christ and His Word.' To be honest, I was unprepared for the initial response I received, which although sincere, was a rejection of the agreement.

As a Christian leader, I assumed that anyone aspiring to lead God's people would be willing to surrender to His Lordship in every way. I went on to explain that I wasn't expecting immediate full compliance, but a willingness of heart to surrender, and even that warranted a whole two weeks of reflection on the part of the delegates on whether or not they were willing to consent to this agreement. They liked the idea of leading God's people, but were somewhat reluctant to first be led by God. Most people want to lead, but find it difficult to obey.

The notion of leadership that seeks to lead and is not willing to obey is very problematic, to say the least, and has at its core "self". Benjamin Franklin was accurate when he observed that, 'He that cannot obey, cannot command.' Even Jesus had to surrender to God's headship:

'And being found in appearance as a man, he humbled himself by becoming obedient to death— even death on a cross! ⁹ Therefore God exalted him to the highest place and gave him the name that is above every name, ¹⁰ that at the name of Jesus every knee should bow, in heaven and on earth and under the earth, ¹¹ and every tongue acknowledge that Jesus Christ is Lord, to the glory of God the Father.' Philippians 2:8-11 (NIV)

Most Christians will agree, in principle, with the need to follow Jesus, but it is often difficult to put into practice. Often times, the pressures of secular influence press on the leader to act contrary to his or her core values. It is easier to follow the crowd, than to walk the narrow path we are called to walk as Christians. Yet, it is in walking this path in obedience that we are truly exalted in God.

It is easier to follow the crowd, than to walk the narrow path we are called to walk as Christians. Yet, it is in walking this path in obedience that we are truly exalted in God.

IN HIS FOOTSTEPS

A few months ago, the entire congregation of our church embarked on a 90-day journey through the four gospels. The campaign was called 'In His Footsteps.' During this period, everyone committed to reading a chapter a day starting from Matthew 1. Each person had an opportunity to share, with other members, their reflections on whichever chapter we were currently reading, via a blog site designed specifically for the campaign. The experience was so enriching. I learnt so much as I paced myself through the gospels and benefited from other people's reflections on their journey. Partly the experience served as a refresher on Jesus' style of leadership – a style based on love and sacrifice, which often stood in sharp contrast to secular thinking. Christians are called to walk in the footsteps of Jesus, and it is as we do so that we truly begin to find ourselves as leaders. The great apostle Paul in 1 Corinthians 11:1 (amplified version) made a profound statement, saying, 'Pattern yourselves after me [follow my example], as I imitate and follow Christ [the Messiah].'

The implication of Paul's statement is that, as a leader, he was only worth following for as long as he followed Christ. Essentially, he was saying that any deviation from following Christ nullified his **any deviation from following Christ nullified his mandate to lead.** mandate to lead. Paul, however followed fervently after Christ, and as such, we are still following his leadership today nearly 2,000 years later. Great leaders are first great followers.

One of the purposes of Christ's coming was to show us how to live, and so as Christians, we have the privilege of walking in the footsteps of the greatest leader that ever lived, Jesus. One must admit that it is so much easier to settle for a religious life of worship than to pursue a challenging life as a disciple of Christ, following in His steps. Ken Leech, a Christian socialist and theologian articulates a major concern when he says that, 'Christianity goes dangerously wrong when Christ is only worshipped but not followed.' Although his view might have been influenced by his socialist views, the quote remains true.

Recently, I read the story of the late Hansie Cronje, the South African Cricket captain and probably the most notable Christian in South African sports in his day. In 2004, he was

Great leaders are first great followers.

voted the 11th greatest South African. Cronje was widely viewed as a committed Christian, who always wore a WWJD (What Would Jesus Do?) engraved bracelet. Yet, it later emerged that he had accepted hundreds of thousands of dollars from match fixers, enlisted two other players into his cheating ring, and worse, it was alleged that he even cheated the other players out of half of their agreed payment![3] Though Cronje professed the lordship of Christ, he did not follow in His footsteps. He was later quoted as saying, 'I tried to live a Christian life and walk the way the Lord wanted me to walk...I allowed Satan and the world to dictate terms to me.'[4] His experience is not uncommon; his public profile just meant that his exposure was on the public stage. Christians are called both to worship and to follow in His footsteps. This, of course means constantly battling against the dictates of the devil and worldly influence.

We might recall that when Jesus called Peter and Andrew as recorded in Matthew 4:19, He said to them, 'Follow Me, and I will make you fishers of men.' They both followed His lead and so became founding leaders of the Christian movement. In the course of following, Peter stumbled, but picked himself up and continued to follow. Christian leaders would do well to heed the warning of Oswald Sanders, 'many who aspire to leadership fail because they have never learned to follow,' and decide to be a consistent follower of Christ. This is the key to Christian leadership.

As the disciples followed Jesus everywhere, they learnt to:

- Speak words of exaltation seasoned with grace and kindness
- Act in love to one another and even to their enemies
- Serve one another, even as Jesus served them
- Live sacrificially
- Conduct themselves in a manner consistent with Jesus' character
- Develop in their devotional life
- Be faithful and obedient to the leading of God's Spirit
- Manage conflicts
- Take responsibility, as Jesus took responsibility for the needs of those who followed Him
- Seek the kingdom of God as the primary goal
- Speak out against injustice

The challenge of following Jesus is in the denial of self; to lay down one's own agenda and need for self gratification and to seek the greater good. In the immediate, it requires discipline and a deep-rooted commitment, which ultimately pays off as the leader steps into a realm of divine partnership with Jesus with far-reaching benefits and impact. This was the experience of the disciples and many great Christian leaders.

The great Evangelist, Billy Graham, is a man known to many as 'America's Pastor', with a track record of close association with several American presidents. At the age of 30, he reached a crossroad in his life when his close friend and associate, Charles Templeton, abandoned the faith they both shared in Christ and even went on to ridicule it. Templeton incited him to do the same. Graham admitted it was a trying time in his life because the core of his life and ministry had been shaken. This event happened as he prepared for an evangelistic campaign in Los Angeles, and so he had to make a decision as to whether the Bible could be trusted and, if so, whether he was going to follow it all the way as a rule book for his life. After much deliberation with himself, he felt a release from the Holy Spirit to pray, 'Father, I am going to accept this [the Bible] as Thy Word – by faith! I am going to allow faith to go beyond my intellectual questions and doubts, and I will believe this to be your inspired Word.'[5] It was that Los Angeles campaign that launched him into international prominence. He continued to follow God's word and through his ministry, millions of people have come to know Christ and to accept God's word as truth.

During a crusade in Modesto, California, Graham and his associates were said to have met to discuss the disturbing issues surrounding the lives of well-known evangelists. In a bid to ensure that they did not fall prey to similar predicaments, they decided upon a list of principles undergirded by God's word that each of them would commit to follow in order to ensure they maintained integrity in ministry. That decision paid off over the years as Billy Graham's evangelistic association became known as *the* model for integrity amongst Christian organisations around the world.[6]

THE LEADER'S IDENTITY
'The evening meal was in progress, and the devil had already prompted Judas, the son of Simon Iscariot, to betray Jesus. Jesus knew that the Father had put all things under his power, and that he had come from God and was returning to God; so he got up from the meal, took off his

outer clothing, and wrapped a towel around his waist. After that, he poured water into a basin and began to wash his disciples' feet, drying them with the towel that was wrapped around him.' – John 13:2-5 (NIV)

The scripture above highlights a few things about Jesus the leader. Though highly esteemed and revered, He served His disciples by washing their feet. In those days, the washing of feet was a menial task reserved for servants who would usually come along to wash the feet of their master or as a show of hospitality for the feet of important visitors. As an example for His disciples to emulate, this was powerfully symbolic. As His disciples we can glean some clues as to the essential elements required in order to develop into the type of leader he was, a leader that serves.

In verse 3 of the above text, we learn that:

- Jesus Knew His Potential – 'Jesus knew that the Father had put all things under his power...' - Jesus' estimation of Himself came from the value the father had placed in Him.
- Jesus Knew His Identity – '...and that he had come from God...' - Identity is the anchor of leadership. It serves as a leader's frame of reference, and in Jesus' case, He derived His identity from God the father. His life, actions and all else flowed from that
- He Knew His Destiny – '...and was returning to God...' – Like Jesus, the ultimate end of every Christian leader is to return to God, and keeping this in mind ought to shape every action and decision of the leader.

All Jesus' acts as recorded in these scriptures have at their core His relationship with the Father. His potential, identity and destiny were all linked to God.

PEOPLE-CENTRED LEADERSHIP

Leadership is a people business. Leading is not about resource management, it is about people. If you lose sight of the people, you run the risk of undermining your own leadership.

One of my favourite pastimes is travelling, so when I get the chance to visit a new city, I love to explore the scenery and more importantly the architecture. Doing this gives me a real sense of involvement in the life of the city. On my trips, I usually try to locate the main cathedral or religious building within the city. I remember visiting the chapel that housed Leonardo Da Vinci's famous painting of the Last Supper in Santa Maria delle Grazie, Milan, Italy, and walking away wowed by the sheer beauty of the chapel. In that instance as on many other occasions, I found I was awed and captivated by the architecture, which often times has existed for centuries. However, my feelings are somewhat dimmed as I find myself wondering whether these religious buildings still serve the people as originally intended or if they have been reduced to mere, albeit beautiful, tourist attractions. On too many occasions, it's the latter case; they are rarely places where the whole person is developed.

Why Keep People at the Core of Leadership?
1. People are invaluable.
2. True fulfilment and real significance comes when leaders serve people.
3. There is no leadership without people.
4. Only people can propagate and amplify any vision.
5. A leader's legacy lives on through the people impacted.

Valuing People

Entrepreneur and cosmetic namesake Mary Kay Ash said that. 'Every one of us goes about with an invisible sign hanging from our neck that reads "Make me feel important,"' and so, we gravitate to people who make us feel valued and appreciated.

Peter J. Daniels, an Australian billionaire, wrote of his former teacher Miss Phillips in his book, *Miss Phillips, You Were Wrong.*[7] He wrote of his experiences as a 7-year old boy who was consistently told by his school teacher (Miss Phillips) that he was no good and would not amount to anything because he did not understand the simple basics of reading and writing. What Miss Phillips failed to consider was that his lack of understanding of text did not ultimately mean that there was nothing else of value in him. Thankfully, he recovered from such rejection and through hardwork and determination, went on to become very successful. His story has a happy ending unlike most others.

Often times, we miss out on what can become of the people around us because of our inability to see real potential or value in them. Great leaders are easily recognisable because their fruits are evident. This is not the case with potential leaders. Their value could easily be overlooked because they have not yet evolved to fit our image of leaders. Every person has potential that can be developed. As a rule, people who think highly of the people around them tend to get more from them. It is interesting, but true, that even without saying much, people know when they are truly valued and respected by others. Leaders see beyond people's current situation and capabilities and are able to see what they might be able to do or become. This is why they take chances on people, and in doing so build confidence, which ultimately releases those people to achieve their best.

Valuing people is a skill that can be learnt. It's a skill that I have been able to learn over the years, and I am confident that anyone can learn to do this. Let us now explore some of the ways we can demonstrate and learn to better value others:

1. Develop a high estimation of people –This may require a mental shift and is a perspective that needs to be cultivated. Every person we meet has something of value. If we accept the saying, 'God never creates trash,' then there is definitely value in every person. John Maxwell describes this as 'Seeing everyone as a 10'[8]; this means that everyone has the potential to be excellent at something. That something just needs to be discovered. That each person has intrinsic value must be our starting point and the basis for all interaction with others.

2. Use words and actions to encourage people – Over time, people either rise or fall to the level of our estimation of them. Words of encouragement go a long way in helping people become what they have the potential to be. Positive words help people develop a mental attitude that alters their perception and gives them hope to succeed. However, it's very difficult to express positive words without sincerity. When our words and feelings are in conflict, it is unlikely that the encouragement we bring will have the desired impact. Human relations expert Les Giblin put it this way, 'You can't make the other fellow feel important in your presence if you secretly feel that he

is a nobody.'

3. Offer resources to help equip the people – Like diamonds, people are precious, and like diamonds they need to be worked on if they are to shine. Equipping people could be costly, but it is an essential element of leadership. You could equip people through training courses, books and audio materials. Equipping people in this way helps transform potential into valuable skills.

At this point, I feel it is important to point out how difficult it is to value people, if as a leader you don't believe that you are of value yourself. In other words, you can't give what you don't have. The key to valuing people is to first develop a healthy degree of self esteem, as we project onto others the view we hold of ourselves.

The key to valuing people is to first develop a healthy degree of self esteem, as we project onto others the view we hold of ourselves.

Investing in People
'Then King Rehoboam consulted the elders who stood before his father Solomon while he still lived, and he said, "How do you advise me to answer these people?" [7] *And they spoke to him, saying, "If you will be a servant to these people today, and serve them, and answer them, and speak good words to them, then they will be your servants forever.'* 1 Kings 12:6-7

A cursory reading of the above scripture might cause one to miss the key principle that God is trying to communicate through King Rehoboam's experience.

Kind Rehoboam had just become king in Israel following the death of his late father, King Solomon. In the latter days of King Solomon's reign, the people's suffering increased and, consequently, their discontent grew. Following Rehoboam's ascension to the throne, the people pleaded with him to ease their suffering and promised that if he did, they would serve him. King Rehoboam sought counsel of the wise men who served as advisers to his father. They advised him to be a servant to the people – to attend to their needs, listen to them, speak encouraging words to them and to care for them. They pointed out that if he did so, the people would willingly serve Him forever. The principle they were trying to teach King Rehoboam was that when a leader serves people, they will, in turn, serve you and go further in their service. The true measure of a leader is not the number of people who serve them, but the number of people they serve.

I have learnt that if you take care of people, they will in turn take care of the business, whatever that business might be. Unfortunately, leaders who only seek to take care of the business end up losing both the

The true measure of a leader is not the number of people who serve them, but the number of people they serve.

people and the business. In any organisation, the relationships of the leader must come before the work that needs doing. Taking this approach generally engenders a sense of belonging and comradeship.

Unfortunately, King Rehoboam did not heed the counsel of the elders. Instead he took the advice of his young and inexperienced friends who suggested that he tighten his grip on the people. As he continued to pursue his own self-interest, the people rebelled and he lost control of all tribes of Israel with the exception of Judah. He lost the people and the kingdom.

Loving People

Love has everything to do with leadership. It is one word that encapsulates the Christian leader's motive for action. When I talk about love here, I am not referring to the emotions that fuel our lustful passions; rather, I mean the decision to care about the well-being of another by the giving of one's self in service and consideration to another. Jesus

A leader cannot truly lead people he or she does not genuinely love.

demonstrated this kind of undying love for those He led: 'Having loved his own who were in the world, He loved them to the end' – John 13: 1 (NIV). It was His love for his disciples that caused Him to stoop low and wash their feet. A leader cannot truly lead people he or she does not genuinely love.

When I started out in a leadership position several years ago, I must confess that I did not understand this principle. My leadership in those days was often tainted by my own personal agenda. Even when this was not clear to anyone else around me, God was always quick to point out such instances to me. His aim was not to put me on a guilt trip, but to bring correction. Over the years, He has taught me that the more I love people, the better able I am to lead. This might sound easy, but as I have strived to practice it over the years, I have found that it strikes at the heart of self-interest. Truth be told, that war hasn't been completely won yet.

1 Corinthians 13 is not a Bible scripture that most people will refer to when considering leadership, but I really feel that it does form part of a comprehensive curriculum on leadership development for any leader. It may not be included in any business school's curriculum, but I would wager that many effective leaders will agree that the qualities described in the scripture below are essential in hands-on leadership.

'Love is patient, love is kind. It does not envy, it does not boast, it is not proud. It does not dishonor others, it is not self-seeking, it is not easily angered, it keeps no record of wrongs. ⁶ Love does not delight in evil but rejoices with the truth. It always protects, always trusts, always hopes, always perseveres. Love never fails.' 1 Corinthians 13:4-8 (NIV)

One can hardly go wrong in leading others if one commits to lead by the attributes listed above. Southwest Airlines is famously referred to as the airline that love built.[ix] Herb Kelleher, the founder of the airline, has a reputation as one of America's finest leaders. He managed to build arguably the most successful American airline from scratch on the principle of loving people. For the airline's staff this has meant doing whatever is necessary to ensure the customer's experience is a positive one.

CHAPTER THREE

THE CHARACTER OF A LEADER

'The integrity of the upright guides them.'
– **Proverbs 11:3**

'If I take care of my character,
my reputation will take care of itself.'
– **D. L. Moody**

As a long time student of leadership, I have found that character is one aspect that best shows the full weight of responsibility that comes with leadership. Courtesy of the media, we are well aware of how failures in character have brought about the downfall of many great leaders. Analogous to an iceberg, the hidden aspects of a leader's life are of more significance than aspects that are visible to all. It is said that leadership is character in action, and a leader's character flows from their value system. James Hunter defines character as the 'moral or ethical strength to behave according to proper values and principles.'[1] For a Christian leader, these values are derived from the leader's relationship with God.

Character is derived from the Greek word, 'charakter', which means 'image' or 'to engrave'. This word is used once in the New Testament of the Bible in the book of Hebrews 1:3, in the context of Christ as the express image (character) of God.

When God chooses a leader, He does not overlook their character. It's actually of critical importance to Him. God appointed David as king over His people in Israel because of the integrity of his heart. While Samuel the Prophet was swayed by the physical appearance of the other candidates for the position of king, God judged their character and found them wanting.

'But the Lord said to Samuel, "Do not look at his appearance or at his physical stature, because I have refused him. For the Lord does not see as man sees; for man looks at the outward appearance[charisma], but the Lord looks at the heart[character]."' – 1 Samuel 16:7

Charisma endears a man to people, but character attracts God to a person. Leaders hardly ever fail because of a lack of charisma, but a failure in character has been the downfall of many a leader.

> **Charisma endears a man to people, but character attracts God to a person.**

Dwight L. Moody said, 'Character is what a man is in the dark.' If that is the case, a very important question everyone should ask themselves is, 'Who am I when no one else is with me?'

Unlike potential, which is what you have the capacity to become, character is who you are now. No one ever appoints a person to a position of influence just on the basis of their potential with the expectation that they'll develop the required character later. You might have the potential to lead, but character is a must from the very start. Some people think that character can be developed once a position of leadership has been assumed. In actual fact, the best time to develop one's character is now, **before** taking on a leadership position. Consequently, subordinate leaders are actually best placed to develop their character while they are still in relative obscurity. Character is best developed in the dark and obscure moments of life.

Character is best developed in the dark and obscure moments of life.

Often times, we look at a person's actions in order to judge their character. In actual fact, actions are not necessarily the best judge of character, because character goes beyond a person's actions and reflects a person's inner thoughts, motives and attitudes. To change one's character, a mere change of action will not suffice. I have, on many occasions, tried to correct or improve certain character traits by simply altering my actions and I have always been frustrated. Simply altering my actions hardly ever results in a permanent change. This is why I tend to be sceptical of basing character assessments on singular actions. You need to look deeper.

A LEADER'S MOST PRECIOUS ASSET

General H. Norman Schwarzkopf, a former U.S. Army General, once commented, 'Leadership is a potent combination of strategy and character. But if you must be without one, be without strategy.'[2] As a subordinate leader myself, I wholeheartedly agree. A lapse in strategy is forgivable, but anything that undermines a leader's character is much harder to overlook. Trust flows from consistency in character. Continual breaches in character result in the gradual erosion of trust. Once a consistent character flaw is discovered, every word the leader utters or any action he or she takes must be assessed for trustworthiness. Eventually, this makes the leader's position untenable.

The emphasis placed on character by Southwest Airlines is demonstrated by the organisation's recruitment motto, 'Hire for character, train for skills'; a business principle often associated with Peter Schutz, the former CEO of Porsche. Southwest Airlines believes that it is more difficult to find people of good character than people with skills, so they would rather train and equip people of good character with the required skills. They believe that such people will be more committed and faithful to their vision.

A person of good character will usually exhibit certain other traits, and these are:

INTEGRITY

The word "integrity" speaks of a complete entity. Integrity is the state of being whole; being one with oneself. It is a state in which a person's words and actions consistently align with each other. When we sit exams, many times, we are graded on a scale of A+ to F. With integrity, there is no scale; you are either a person of integrity or not. Every person has the opportunity to prove their integrity. Doing exactly what you said you would do, keeping your word, and doing the right thing when no one is looking all show a person's integrity. Habits such as turning up late for appointments, telling little white lies, or making empty promises may seem insignificant, but they say a lot about a person's integrity. Max Depree, an outstanding Christian businessman and author, remarks, 'Integrity in all things precedes all else.'

When we sit exams, many times, we are graded on a scale of A+ to F. With integrity, there is no scale; you are either a person of integrity or not.

Integrity is not a matter for work or ministry alone; it affects every part of one's life. I remember being called upon to settle a marital dispute that arose between a couple in my church some time ago. One of the issues the wife raised centered on integrity. She made statements such as, 'My husband lies and makes empty promises to me and the kids.' In her frustration, she lashed out with the words, 'In fact, I do not trust my husband and if I was told that my husband wanted to kill me, I would believe it.' Now, if this seems extreme to you, you'd be right. I know her husband and I know that he is not the kind of person who would ever consider such a devilish act, but the problem was that trust had been eroded and integrity had been breached. Once that happens, people are able to believe the worst about people they once respected or even loved. I sat the husband down and explained these facts to him, and he has since started to make deliberate changes, which his wife now happily attests to. Slowly, trust is being rebuilt.

An informal survey of the CEOs of a number of major companies was conducted by Henry and Richard Blackaby. [3] The survey asked these CEOs what they looked for in potential employees and the majority cited integrity as the number one qualification. Employers are not the only people that look out for integrity; subordinates and peers seek it in those that lead them, too.

FAITHFULNESS

Mother Theresa is known worldwide because of her work with the 'poorest of the poor' in Calcutta, India. I am often amazed at how such work, which one would expect to be obscured from the eyes of the world, managed to gain the attention of world leaders across the globe.

Giving herself so fully to people who could not reciprocate her gesture required Mother Theresa to be faithful to her purpose. This is a fact that she herself acknowledged when she said, 'I do not pray for success, I ask for faithfulness.' She might not have prayed for success, but her faithfulness earned her global recognition. Faithfulness is one of God's conditions for promotion. Jesus Christ expressed this sentiment in the parable of the talents as recorded in the Bible: 'And he said to him, "Well done, good servant! Because you have been faithful in a very little, you shall have authority over ten cities,"' – Luke 19:17 (ESV)

Being faithful is an attitude required of all leaders. 'Moreover it is required in stewards that a man be found faithful' – 1 Corinthians 4:2 (KJV). People who are faithful usually stay the course and are very reliable. All leaders look for faithful people to propagate and amplify their vision. Julia Ward Howe, the American writer, poet and social activist, said that, 'whilst ambitious people only seek to climb up, faithful people seek to build up.'

The apostle Paul recognised that in propagating a vision, faithful men were a sure medium. Hence, his advice to Timothy, 'and what you have heard from me in the presence of many witnesses entrust to faithful men who will be able to teach others also' – 2 Timothy 2:2 (ESV).

ACCOUNTABILITY

I remember attending a meeting some years back wherein all the attendees were asked to introduce themselves and to say who they were accountable to. It was a question I had never considered before. Attendees cited their spouses, children, bosses, colleagues and those within their community as people to whom they were accountable. When my turn came, I responded that I was accountable to my spouse and to my senior pastor. Since then, I have given the question more thought and have added three more personalities to the list of those to whom I have made myself liable to give account. They are God, my sister and my child.

Everyone should have at least one other person they are accountable to – a person to whom they owe an explanation for every action or decision they make. Being accountable is important because it keeps you on the straight and narrow, and in many ways helps you to keep a check on your motives.

I remember giving my wife the names of two people she could speak to in the event that I refused to consider her viewpoint, or if she observed unexplainable behaviour. I have intentionally made myself accountable to these people in order to keep myself in check and to prevent any bad or unacceptable behaviour on my part.

Beyond committing to providing an explanation to one's accountability partners, every Christian leader has a duty to be transparent and accountable to God. This is necessary, because the deeper issues of life exist within the 'thought realm'. This is an area to which no one but God has free access. He knows our every thought and move, and so it is foolish to hide away from Him.

'...All things are naked and open to the eyes of Him to whom we must give account.' – *Hebrews 4:13*

From the scriptural account of Joseph's reaction to Potiphar's wife's overtures, we can discern that he was accountable to God. When she proposed that he lay with her, he rejected her offer, not just because of his loyalty to his master, which would be laudable enough, but on the grounds that God was watching his every move and he could not commit such a sin against God (Genesis 39:9). In my personal attempts to be accountable to God, I am making it a practice to be conscious of the fact that He is reading my every thought and watching my every move.

DEVELOPING CHARACTER
If you find yourself dismaying at the state of your character, be encouraged; the good news is that character can be developed, and so, no one is at a permanent disadvantage in the quest to develop the necessary leadership virtues described above. It is challenging, but well worth it and certainly achievable.

When it comes to leading, character development is a non-negotiable. If one fails to develop in character now, it is bound to show up at a later date in an unexpected situation and place. Our God-given ability to mould our own character should encourage us. One might not be able to choose one's place of birth and the family into which one is born; however, we can mould our character if we choose to. Henry David Thoreau said, 'I know of no more encouraging fact than the unquestionable ability of man to elevate his life by conscious endeavour.' Character formation takes conscious endeavour.

The road to godly character is known to many, but walked by few. This is simply because it is easier to know what is right than to do what is right. It is walking this rarely worn path that distinguishes a true leader. Many years ago, I decided to set off on this path, and admittedly, it has been a running battle. Every victory gained, though hard on the flesh, has made me a better person. Like everything else, character is developed in the same way habits are formed. Human beings are known to be creatures of habit, and so anything that becomes part of our subconscious programming determines our every thought and action. We become what we repeatedly do.

The road to godly character is known to many, but walked by few.

The starting point for character development is God's word and an awareness of God's presence watching over our every thought and action. Joseph understood this well. It was his consciousness of God's presence that kept him diligent during his period of service to both Potiphar and Pharaoh. This consciousness helped Joseph refuse the advances of Potiphar's wife.

MATTERS OF THE HEART

Forming a habit of godly character is a great achievement that does bear fruits. Since character can often be a moving target that one never quite arrives at, there is an ongoing need for alignment. God does this by nudging at the door of a leader's heart to take the leader to another level of conformity to His image through obedience. In the book, *Leaders on Leadership*, Jack Hayford wrote in his chapter on the character of a leader that, 'A leader's character will never rise beyond the flow level of his obedience to the Holy Spirit's dealings with the heart.'[4] This implies that a tender heart is required as proof of willingness so that the Holy Spirit can continually realign our response in accordance to God's leading.

DEVELOPING THROUGH CHALLENGES

Challenges are one of life's constants. Whether big or small, easy or difficult, we all go through challenges at one point or the other. They help to both reveal and to form one's character. When we go through a challenge, our real self is revealed. The way a person handles these difficulties says a lot about a person's character. Challenges can either make a person bitter or better.

> **Challenges can either make a person bitter or better.**

When faced with a challenge, one could choose to see it as an opportunity upon which to build character or choose to compromise their character in order to avoid the challenge. Building our character through tough times is a choice we make. When we seek shortcuts, we miss out on the best opportunities to develop character.

CHAPTER FOUR

COMPETENCIES (SKILLS) OF A LEADER

'He cared for them with a true heart and led them with skilful hands.' – Psalm 78:72 (NLT)

'A competent leader can get efficient service from poor troops, while on the contrary an incapable leader can demoralize the best of troops.' – John J. Pershing

I came into my current pastoral role at Trinity Chapel, RCCG in 2005 because the two pastors who had responsibility for this function were leaving the church. They had been commissioned to set up new churches. Their absence meant there was a pressing need for pastoral staff. My predecessors were true pastors at heart and had done such wonderful jobs of overseeing the growing pastoral needs of the 700 or so members of the church at that time. At the time, I felt that the shoes I was required to fill were too big for me and I struggled in the role. My self-doubt was compounded by the comments of a respected (and no doubt well-meaning) mentor who told me that he could not imagine me functioning successfully in the role. Thankfully, during the many years of serving in this capacity, I have developed and continue to develop the skills needed to meet the pastoral needs of the church and also lead the growing number of volunteers who give their time in serving the vision of the church.

A competent leader is one who possesses the required skills, knowledge, qualifications and capacity needed to lead effectively. Starting out as a leader with *positional* authority, I wasn't a competent leader right away. I had to learn the competencies required for me to execute the role effectively. I had to earn the right to lead. In the book of Samuel, we learn that David was not just a man who reflected God's heart in caring for His people, but also one with great ability to turn distressed, indebted and discontented men (1 Samuel 22:2) into mighty and highly motivated warriors (2 Samuel 23:8-39). David didn't start out that way, he developed those skills during his wilderness years.

Like all leadership attributes, the competencies of a leadership role can be learned, through committed practice and repetition. Leaders are primarily self-developing. The best leaders work on

The best leaders work on themselves continually, learning, growing, and becoming more capable and competent over time.

themselves continually, learning, growing, and becoming more capable and competent over time. A leader's competence is developed daily; it is bought on a 'time-payment plan', with a new instalment required each day.[1]

Gifts are different from competence. Whilst gifts are natural talents, competence has to be developed. Michael Jordan, a former American professional basketball player, once said that, 'everybody has talent, but ability takes hard work. What Michael Jordan was implying was that talent is not enough to succeed and that a concerted effort to develop one's talent into well honed skill is required. Developing the competencies necessary for leadership requires hard work, but the payoff is always worth the effort.

Leadership competencies mainly take two forms, namely:
- Relational Competencies – Soft Skills
- Technical Competencies – Hard Skills

RELATIONAL COMPETENCIES – SOFT SKILLS
Relational competencies encompass those skills that help a leader connect with people either on a one-on-one basis, within a group or with an audience. To succeed as a leader, one must work with and through others, and to do that most effectively, it is essential to learn how to connect with people. Charles Schwab is said to have been the first person to earn an annual salary of $1 million. As an employee of Andrew Carnegie, the deceased American steel billionaire of the early 20th century, Schwab was paid this amount of money because of his ability to connect with people in a way that delivered

results for Carnegie.[2] Excellent relational skills stem from a genuine interest in others, the desire to understand people, and the choice to prioritised positive interactions with others.

Relational competencies include:

1. Communication – This competency encompasses the exchange of ideas, thoughts and opinions through various means, such as spoken, written and electronic media. According to a Harvard Business Review article, the ability to communicate effectively is regarded as the number one criteria for advancement and promotion for professionals. [3] To lead effectively in any capacity, communication is very important.

'For if the trumpet makes an uncertain sound, who will prepare for battle?' – 1 Corinthians 14:8

In most relationships, clear, consistent and courteous communication usually fuels the right action. Leaders are always on the lookout for progress, and not just any progress, but progress in the right direction, towards a desired goal. Communication helps to achieve this. As such, communication is probably the most important competency of an effective leader. John W. Gardner, a teacher on the subject of leadership, summed up the importance of communication when he said, 'If I had to name a single, all-purpose instrument of leadership, it would be communication.'

Effective communication is a two-way street, namely:
- Active listening – seeking first to understand the situation and the person

- Speech, writing or signs – capturing the heart and the mind in a way that necessitates the right action

The position occupied by a subordinate leader within an organisation means that he or she has to learn 'effective multi-stream communication: upwards with the lead leader, sideways with colleagues and downwards with subordinates.

2. Conflict Resolution – Living and working amicably with others and creating an environment in which others can do likewise is a key competency of leadership. Whilst it is impossible for people to always agree on every matter, resolving differences is necessary in order to maintain healthy relationships and to keep a concerted focus on the goal. Conflict could arise out of differences in opinion, personality clashes, a lack of team spirit, poor communication, office politics and poor planning, to name but a few causes. Further, it is inevitable, as Jim Van Yperen said, 'If death and taxes are the first two certainties of life, conflict is the third.' [4]

The lead leader often enjoys the privilege of choosing who he or she works with, but in most cases the subordinate leader does not have that luxury. As a result, the middle-tier leaders within an organisation have to learn to negotiate disagreements in a way that recognises mutual rights and intelligence of all those involved and leads to a harmonious solution. [5]

As a subordinate leader, I have, on many occasions, had to resolve conflicts between myself and others and also resolve issues between others. I have learnt that only few conflicts are unresolvable. Further in most cases the parties involved can be reconciled. When resolving conflicts, leaders look for common ground or interests as the starting point for resolution, with the hope of securing a win-win for all the parties embroiled in the conflict. Whilst it might not be possible to totally eradicate conflict, it can be minimised by ensuring that the following are adopted:

1. Clearly defined roles, responsibilities and expectations
2. Creation of opportunities for grievances to be addressed, either publicly or privately
3. Where possible, only those who fit the existing team culture should be employed
4. Fostering a team spirit through regular team-building exercises
5. Deliberate focus on the shared vision
6. Close observation of the team dynamics

When conflict does arise, the leader needs to:
1. Address the issues as soon as possible
2. Listen to all parties concerned
3. Maintain objectivity in decision making
4. Engage all parties in reaching an amicable solution

TECHNICAL COMPETENCIES – HARD SKILLS
1. Vision – This refers to the clear mental picture of a preferred future. It is something seen in the realm of the imagination that is yet to become a reality. Vision casting is a key function of leadership, without which a leader cannot take others on a journey. If a leader cannot see where he is going, he is unlikely to

If a leader cannot see where he is going, he is unlikely to get there himself never mind getting others there.

get there himself never mind getting others there. A clear vision is critical for the success of any team or organisation. It, therefore, stands to reason that leaders must be visionaries. [6]

Where does a leader's vision come from? Christians believe that true vision comes from God. Secular leaders would argue that setting a vision is a human activity. Whilst Noah's vision to build the ark was a remarkable God-given vision (Genesis 6), Bill Gates' legendary vision of every computer in the world running Microsoft Windows is also very inspiring.

Once the vision is clearly defined, leaders expend major resources in order to ensure that the people buy into the vision. A clear and inspiringly delivered vision causes people to own the vision. Once a subordinate leader is able to own the vision, it becomes easier to see his or her role in realizing the vision.

The first thing I do when I take on a new team is to define the vision of the team in the context of the wider vision of the church or organisation. The question a subordinate leader should always ask is, 'What will this vision look like from the perspective of my own team?' Once this is known, it should be communicated repeatedly and in different forms to all team members. Andy Stanley often says that 'vision leaks'; as such, it is necessary to continually reiterate the vision.

Remaining true to the overall vision is a real challenge for a subordinate leader. This is explored further in chapter 7 of this book.

2. Planning – Having a vision is one thing; realising it is quite another thing. Planning is the bridge that links the vision to reality. Leaders understand that if they fail to plan, they plan to fail. Planning is, therefore, essential to ensure realisation of the vision.

A few years ago, I had the privilege of spending some time with Pastor Sunday Adelaja in Ukraine. He is the pastor of the largest church in Europe. During one of our many sessions together, he mentioned that he always prepares at least three alternate ways of achieving any goal or vision. This level of thought in the planning **Planning helps ensure that success is more probable.** process ensures that if one approach fails, there are still other means of reaching the desired goal. Planning helps ensure that success is more probable.

Over the years, I have come to realise that the more I plan, the more successful my efforts are. I also recognise that the goal of planning is not necessarily to create a finished plan. Rather, the planning process affords one the opportunity to think through the critical elements and steps necessary to achieve the desired goal. General Dwight Eisenhower once said that, 'plans are nothing, but the planning is everything.'

I subscribe to the rule of thumb that, 'Every minute spent in planning saves 10 minutes in execution.' When planning, you must begin with the end goal (the vision) in mind. The vision should be broken down into a series of smaller achievable goals. These smaller goals should be broken down into actionable tasks. Each of these tasks can then be assigned to each team member. This allows each member to take responsibility for the delivery of an aspect of the vision, which reinforces a sense of common ownership. Effective planning also helps you identify which tasks can be performed in parallel and which ones need to be done sequentially. This can help you make the best use of the available time.

As a leader, including your team in the planning process increases your chances of success. The involvement of your team members will almost certainly eradicate possible resistance during the execution phase because, 'those who plan the battle hardly battle the plan.'

3. Problem Solving – Problem solving is the practice of finding and applying solutions to challenges and hindrances that stand in the way of achieving a desired goal. In *How the Best Leaders Lead*, Brian Tracy says, 'A goal unachieved is merely a problem unsolved.' The level of success of any leader is dependent on the problems the leader is able to solve.

> **The level of success of any leader is dependent on the problems the leader is able to solve.**

As a subordinate leader, I have learnt that my role only exists because there is a problem that needs to be solved. Joseph was hired by Pharaoh to solve the problem of food management (storage and distribution) in Egypt (Genesis 41:33-41). In my case, one of the problems I was hired to solve is the management of the care needs of the members within the church. Do you know what problem you were hired to solve?

The first thing leaders need to do when faced with a problem is to take responsibility for solving it. As a subordinate leader, I have found that lead leaders are more inclined to work with people who not only identify a problem, but also present different ways of solving the problem. Problem solving is an essential competency of leadership and most assuredly secures a subordinate leader's role.

The following practices will help with the process of exploring problems and identifying possible solutions:

1. Clearly understand what the real problem is, not just the symptoms.
2. Communicate the problem to the team.
3. Concentrate single-mindedly on the problem.
4. Consider various ways of solving the problem and identify the risks associated with each option.

5. Create a systematic, step-by-step and easy-to-implement plan for solving the problem.
Continually evaluate the solution you delivered to ensure that it has effectively solved the problem.

4. Prioritizing – The ability to determine which a multitude of tasks requires most of the available resources is a skill that leaders must develop. To prioritise means to designate a task as more important than other things.

The task or goal which is prioritised above all else by an organisation usually flows from the core values of the organisation. For a subordinate leader to effectively prioritise work, he or she must have a good understanding of the core values of the organisation. It is also important to recognise that the lead leader's priorities often determine those of the subordinate's own priorities. Therefore, to know what to prioritise, it is always helpful to ask the lead leader the simple question, 'What three things am I required to do that are more important to you than anything else I might do?' Once these priorities are clearly defined, get to work on prioritizing those three things. That doesn't mean you should neglect the other things that need doing, however, those other tasks shouldn't take up as much of your resources.

Leaders take a similar approach to their own personal development; that is they prioritise around their individual values. The ability to master the following steps will improve a leader's effectiveness:

1.   Define your core values.
2.   Order your life according to these values.
3.   Discipline your life around these values.

The secret of a leader's success is in what he or she prioritises daily.

The level of development of the competencies cited here will vary from person to person but all of them can be developed. There are four main ways by which these competencies can be developed, and they are through:

The secret of a leader's success is in what he or she prioritises daily.

1.   Education and training
2.   Experience gained on the job
3.   Self-discipline to improve performance
4.   Mentoring by more competent leaders

CHAPTER FIVE

CONSEQUENCES OF LEADERSHIP

'Therefore I do not run like someone running
aimlessly; I do not fight like a boxer beating the air.
No, I strike a blow to my body and make it my slave
so that after I have preached to others, I myself will
not be disqualified for the prize.'
1 Corinthians 9:26-27 (NIV)

'The brighter the persona, the darker the shadow.'
– Carl Jung

Consequence is a word often associated with negativity. However, in this chapter, it is used in its purest form – the results or outcomes of particular actions. One of John Maxwell's most notable quotes is, 'Everything rises and falls on leadership.' I have come to accept this as a fundamental truth in leadership – leading comes with great consequences. Great wars have been won as a result of exemplary leadership; nations have been built, great organisations formed, successful families raised, and great ministries established, all due to leaders that have raised the leadership bar and have lived lives that have inspired others. The converse is also true. There are 'leaders' in all spheres of life who, due to one failing or another, have torn down the great work they were doing. Failures in leadership have led to the collapse of great multinationals, such as Enron, the American energy giant and the recent closure of the News of the World, a British tabloid. In Christian ministry, some leaders have made a shipwreck of their ministries and brought God's name into disrepute as a result of their moral failures. The effect of a leader's actions is often further reaching than we might imagine.

As Carl Jung said, 'The brighter the persona, the darker the shadow.' The impact of a leader's leadership casts shadows over those they lead, both positively and negatively. Leaders **Leaders that have led well cast shadows of hope, aspiration and trust.** that have led well cast shadows of hope, aspiration and trust. Others leave their followers groping in dark despair and suspicion.

Leading has rewards for the leader, but also pitfalls, which impact the leader as well as those led. The apostle Paul in the Bible was a leader who understood the consequences of leadership. He understood the impact of his leadership on others and he was not fooled into thinking himself infallible. He knew the dangers that leaders often face and he was determined to overcome them at all cost to prevent himself from being disqualified from leading. Being aware of the rewards and pitfalls of leadership will help to better equip the subordinate leader for more senior leadership designation.

In *Overcoming the Dark Side of Leadership*, Gary McIntosh and Samuel Rima unravelled a striking paradox: it is the very thing that compels people to aspire for success that also precipitates their failure. [1] In the next few sections, we will consider both the rewards and the pitfalls of leadership.

REWARDS OF LEADERSHIP

Material Benefits
Every position has its privileges and, there are usually many perks that accompany leadership positions. While leaders ought not to pursue these positions for the material benefits; such perks do allow one to be a bit more comfortable and as a result more focused on pursuing the interests of the organisation.

This is why in 1 Corinthians 9, the apostle Paul admonished Christians in Corinth on the need to meet the material needs of those who serve them. Proverbs 27:23-27 (NIV) also provides a helpful perspective of the benefits of leadership roles:

'Be sure you know the condition of your flocks, give careful attention to your herds; for riches do not endure forever, and a crown is not secure for all generations.

When the hay is removed and new growth appears and the grass from the hills is gathered in, the lambs will provide you with clothing, and the goats with the price of a field. You will have plenty of goats' milk to feed your family and to nourish your female servants.'

Leaders benefit in different ways from those they lead. Material benefits, such as money, and gifts are all very attractive, but subordinate leaders should not get carried away by these things. If the driving force for aspiring to a leadership role is the material benefits, you'll be short-changed as it will soon become apparent that the weight of responsibility often outweighs the benefits. You have to be motivated by more than material gain.

Power
Material benefit is not the only thing that people find attractive about leadership. The power that leaders exert is another factor that endears leadership to people. The power wielded by the senior leader gives him or her freedom to act, and thus gives them greater influence over the direction of the events around them and by extension the direction of the organisation.

Power is a permission given to a leader by the people he or she leads, which gives the leader the ability to influence them. Like money, power is 'value neutral' in that it is neither good nor bad rather; its impact is dependent on the person wielding it. A leader's power should serve as a force for good. Jesus demonstrated this through his three years of ministry on earth, the impact of which still reverberates today.

Leaders face a choice between exercising positional power, which is as a result of their position, or relational power, which is based on the relationships they have built within the organisation. Great leaders choose to lead based on relational power.

The major downside to power is excellently expressed in the famous Lord Acton's quote, 'Power tends to corrupt, and absolute power corrupts absolutely.' Having unbiased structures of accountability helps overcome this downside.

Popularity

In the Bible, David's opportunity came to light in the shadow of King Saul. His exploits on the battlefield against Goliath brought him popularity and caused the people to sing his praises.

'As they danced, they sang: "Saul has slain his thousands, and David his tens of thousands."' 1 Samuel 18:7 (NIV)

A leader's effectiveness in delivering results often causes the leader to grow in popularity. Herb Kelleher, the acclaimed co-founder of Southwest Airlines, was so popular with his 16,000-strong staff that they raised $60,000 among themselves and took out a full-page advert in 1994 in *USA Today* to demonstrate their appreciation of him on Boss's Day. [2, 3] Such a public display of affection is gratifying for any leader.

However leaders need to remember that leadership is not a popularity contest. It is possible for those who celebrated a leader's former success to be willing **Leaders do what** to cast stones at the very same leader **is right and not** when he or she makes unpopular **necessarily what** decisions. Leaders do what is right **is popular.** and not necessarily what is popular.

In the case of subordinate leaders, being popular could present a challenge, particularly if the subordinate becomes more popular than the main leader. This was the experience of David, who incurred the wrath of King Saul as a result of his growing popularity following his military exploits. Often times, insecure leaders feel threatened by a subordinate's popularity and might seek to get rid of their perceived competitors. Consequently this is a situation that a subordinate leader must handle wisely. We learn a lesson from David's response to Saul's antics; David recognised that God had placed King Saul over him, and so, he looked to God to deal with the situation. He had to keep a low profile for a period of time whilst God dealt with the situation. David became a better leader as a result. God should always be our starting point if found in any such situation.

Prestige
Certain honour is accorded to leaders by virtue of the position they hold. This gives the leader a reputation that commands the respect of others.

The Bible teaches that leaders who rule well deserve honour:

'Let the elders who rule well be considered worthy of double honour, especially those who labor in preaching and teaching.' 1 Timothy 5:17 (ESV)

'Give to everyone what you owe them: Pay your taxes and government fees to those who collect them, and give respect and honour to those who are in authority.' Romans 13:7 (NLT)

The respect accorded a leader often means that people will want to follow the leader, associate themselves with him or her, heed the leader's words, and even seek to please the leader. All these make the role of a leader a desirable one to most people. Usually, this honour is linked to the office of the leader. In other words, anyone who holds that particular position or office will receive such honour. However, it is also necessary for the occupier of such an office to live up to the respect accorded their office; otherwise, they lose the respect.

The world places a premium on status, but true leaders recognise its actual value. [4] The danger of prestige is that it can plays on a leader's ego. In other words you start to 'believe your own hype'. When this happens it often precipitates the leader's downfall.

Fulfilment

Beyond material benefits and the accolades people pay to leaders, there is a deep inner sense of fulfilment when a leader is making a real impact in the lives of those affected by his or her leadership. This is especially the case when one's motives were altruistic.

Nehemiah took it upon himself to rebuild the walls of Jerusalem. In doing so, he also rebuilt the confidence and security of a people that had suffered the loss of almost all they possessed. The results of Nehemiah's various reforms were so fulfilling for him that he felt it was appropriate to mention his accomplishments before God. He closed the book by saying:

'Remember me with favor, my God.' – *Nehemiah 13:14 (NIV)*

It is this very sense of fulfilment that Abraham Maslow defined as man's greatest need. He termed it, 'the need for self-actualization'. It is the sense that God is looking down upon our efforts as leaders, with pleasure. This cannot be quantified in material terms. Apostle Paul expressed this deep sense of fulfilment thus, 'I have fought the good fight, I have finished the race, I have kept the faith. Now there is in store for me the crown of righteousness, which the Lord, the righteous Judge, will award to me on that day – and not only to me, but also to all who have longed for His appearing' – 2 Timothy 4:7-8.

PITFALLS OF LEADERSHIP

Every now and again, we hear of leaders who have made a shipwreck of their lives, organisations or the lives of their followers. The nature of leadership is such that when it fails, it invariably leaves a trail of disappointments in its wake.

However, pitfalls can be avoided. Identifying potential pitfalls before they are encountered can help subordinate leaders become aware that they are equally susceptible to them.

Pride/Ego

Abraham Lincoln said, 'Nearly all men can stand adversity, but if you want to test a man's character, give him power.' As a man who attained one of the highest offices of leadership, that of the president of the United States, he understood how power reveals a person's real character. Leadership roles do not make people proud or egotistical; they merely reveal the real person.

Leadership roles do not make people proud or egotistical; they merely reveal the real person.

Pride is having an inordinately high opinion of one's self. It is that sense of being better, above and more privileged than others. It creates a disconnection between the leader and those they lead, and that, in itself, defeats the purpose of Godly leadership. It disguises itself in many forms, such as being unteachable, robbing others of the credit due to them, a belief in one's infallibility, self-sufficiency and being condescending to others, to name a few.

Personally, pride was a pitfall that God kept pointing out in my own life. He made me understand that He could not entrust me with leadership as long as I continued to look down on others. God takes a stand against proud people. Scripture records that God resists the proud (Proverbs 16:5, James 4:6). Pride makes it difficult for a leader to receive help from others, including from God, because he or she feels that their own way is better than any other way. It was pride that made God move against Nebuchadnezzar, the king of Babylon in the fourth chapter of the book of Daniel in the Bible. Nebuchadnezzar's became proud because of the greatness and expanse of his kingdom and so he refused to acknowledge God. God showed Himself sovereign and all-powerful by causing Nebuchadnezzar to take a leave of his senses for a time, living out in the fields like an animal. Pride is at the root of the downfalls of many great leaders, and it is one that every subordinate leader should guard against.

The danger with pride is how insidious it is. It sneaks up on you. Often, even when it is obvious to those around, it maybe unnoticed by its victim. Oswald Sanders in *Spiritual Leadership* [5] highlighted three tests that can aid the identification of this pitfall, namely:
1. The test of precedence – How do we react when another is preferred in our stead?
2. The test of sincerity – How do we feel when others point out our obvious weaknesses?
3. The test of criticism – When criticised, do we become resentful or do we justify ourselves?

Selfish Ambition
It is necessary for leaders to have drive, a keenness to aspire to great things and a desire to take their people somewhere better than their current state. This is very different from the selfish ambition that causes a leader to be driven by their own personal will to succeed, often at the expense of those being led. Being selfless is a trait that characterises great leaders. Our natural bent is towards self gratification, and so it is very easy to become ambitious in a self-seeking way.

Selfish ambition can result in scheming, politicking, gossiping and creating divisions within organisations. Selfish leaders always leave chaos and disorder in their wake.[6] Absalom, King David's son, was driven by selfish ambition, which led him to conspire to overthrow his father as king over Israel (2 Samuel 15).

For most people, their selfish ambition may not be as dramatic as Absalom, yet it is nevertheless a pitfall to look out for. For the Christian leader, it often disguises itself as a desire to do something great and better for the kingdom of God. Leaders that take time to examine themselves are able to spot the signs of selfish ambition. Signs include criticism of the presiding leader, holding the view that you'd perform better in that role. Learning to admit selfish ambition, and not giving it room to grow, is the first step to overcoming this pitfall.

Moral Failure
I am amazed but thankful that God chose to expose the stumblings of leaders in the Bible. This has provided us with the opportunity to learn from their experiences. Moral failure appears to be a slippery one for biblical leaders, and it is one which still afflicts leaders today. We only need to watch the news to realise how prevalent moral failures are amongst both Christian and secular leaders.

From a Christian point of view, moral failure is defined as departing from one's core convictions of right and wrong as rooted in the Bible. Moral failures often relate to the misappropriation of money, sexual relations and power. The Bible describes moral failures in these three areas as the lust of the flesh, the lust of the eyes and the pride of life (1 John 2:16).

The higher one rises in the leadership hierarchy, the greater one's susceptibility to moral failure. These failings can destroy reputations, careers and families. From the subordinate leader's position it is easy to overlook this potential pitfall while taking the moral high ground and passing judgement on senior leaders who stumble in this area. As a result they do, not see the need to address the same issue in their own lives.

Subordinate leaders can avoid this pitfall by proactively putting safeguards in place. The renowned evangelist, Billy Graham overcame these moral failures by building specific safeguards into his personal and professional life in order to ensure that he and his team were able to avoid compromise. One such safeguard was that Billy Graham never met, travelled, or ate alone with any woman other than his wife. To ensure strict adherence to these safeguards, he set up accountability structures to monitor himself. To some, these are extreme measures. However, such radical actions are sometimes required if one is to live above the reproach of moral failures.

Busy Lives

In the UK, the average full-time work week is 37 hours, with a fifth of workers in Britain working more than 45 hours a week. These figures are much worse in other developed countries such as the United States, Australia and Japan.[7] I know of a significant number of people who regularly work in excess of 60 hours a week. When asked why they work so many hours, apart from the argument that there is always so much to do, another oft-given reason is that to do less hours would give the boss the impression that he or she is a lazy and unfit for the work demands of the organisation. Consequently, many subordinates seek to impress their boss by working extra long hours and taking on a workload that is often detrimental to other important elements of their lives.

According to the same fact sheet quoted above, trends in UK working hours by the Office for National Statistics in

2003 found that those working the longest hours in the UK were men, often with children, aged between 30 and 49. The pressure this puts on their families, in particular their children, is often not known until much later in the lives of the children. As a child, I grew up with a dad who worked 12-14 hours a day. This meant that my father and I did not really start to form a close relationship until much later in life after his retirement. However, by this time, he had missed out on the formative years of my life.

Many Christian leaders will list their relationship with God as their number one priority; however it is highly unlikely that an excessive workload will allow anyone to cultivate a healthy relationship with God. In such instances, one of the first things to be neglected is our personal devotional time, activities such as Bible studying/reading, praying, meditation and other spiritual disciplines. When leaders allow their daily commitments to crowd out their time with God, they are slowly cutting themselves off from their lifeline. [8]

While we might all agree to the importance of keeping our devotional life alive, we rarely do enough to prevent our busy work lives from choking it out. As Stephen Covey said, 'The main thing is to keep the main thing the main thing.' One has to learn to prioritise in order to make room for the 'main' things in life. Jesus put it this way, 'But seek first the kingdom of God and his righteousness, and all these things will be added to you' – Matthew 6:33 (ESV).

The Praise and Approval of Men

The praise of men is a snare for most leaders and particularly for subordinate leaders whose performance is defined and assessed by the senior leader. Whilst it is important that we perform our duties and also seek to build relationships with others around us, it becomes problematic when we act in ways that betray our values in order to gain the approval of men.

Jesus spoke concerning the praise of men in many instances in scriptures. In one episode, recorded in Matthew 23:5, He said concerning the religious leaders of his day (Pharisees and Scribes), 'But all their works they do to be seen by men.' The apostle Paul said in Galatians 1:10, 'For do I now persuade men, or God? Or do I seek to please men? For if I pleased men, I would not be a bondservant of Christ.' It is impossible to be a 'man pleaser' and please God at the same time. Sometimes, as Paul noted in the scripture above, to remain true to God, we may have to stand alone.

Aaron was Moses' assistant, who bowed to pressure from the people when they asked for alternative gods to be made (See Exodus 32). Saul lost his kingship because he 'feared the people and obeyed their voice,' rather than obey God (1 Samuel 15:24). Neither Aaron nor Saul experienced the fullness of their call because they sought men's approval rather than pleasing God.

There will always be differing opinions on most issues, and leaders should learn not to bow to the pressure of people.

As stated elsewhere in this book, leadership is all about people and without people following, one is not really leading. So in order to keep people following, leaders are prone to bowing to the pressure of their people for fear of being deserted or opposed. In his book, *Dealing with Rejection and Praise of Man*, Bob Sorge said, 'The one you fear is the one you will seek to please.' [9]

Leaders are so called because they do the right things and not necessarily what is popular. There will always be differing opinions on most issues, and leaders should learn not to bow to the pressure of people.

CHAPTER SIX

BUILDING INFLUENCE

'Then King Rehoboam consulted the elders who
stood before his father Solomon while he still lived,
and he said, "How do you advise me to answer these
people?" And they spoke to him, saying, "If you will
be a servant to these people today, and serve them,
and answer them, and speak good words to them,
then they will be your servants forever."'
1 Kings 12:6-7

'Leadership is Influence
– nothing more, nothing less.'
– John C Maxwell.

One of the first things that I learnt about leadership
is that to lead, one needs to be able to influence
people. I learnt that while I may
hold a leadership position with one or **Leadership is**
more people reporting to me, the position **really the**
does not guarantee that they will follow **specific**
my lead. I had to develop the ability to **application**
influence, because you *influence* people **of influence**.

into following you. Leadership is really the specific application of influence.

In paid employment, positional leadership often works better than it does in volunteer-based organisations. Consequently, it is easy to labour under the delusion that those who report to us are following because of our leadership competence often times, this is not the case. In most organisations, people do their work because they are paid to do so (and have bills to pay!), not because they have been effectively influenced to do so. You may want to ask yourself this question: 'Would my subordinates work with me if they were doing it in a voluntary capacity, if their need for money were not a factor?' I once heard a quote that resonated with me; it goes as follows, 'It is a bad day for a leader when he or she has to lead from positional authority.' The best leaders lead, not out of positional authority, but through the influence they have with their people. It is certainly true that you don't have to hold a position to lead. What you need to have is influence. Influence can have a multi-directional effect reaching those above you, those on the same level as you and your subordinates.

Influence is a prized commodity in leadership; without it, there is no success. Influence is like a force that moves or impels a person or people to action.

We all have influence with people and are equally subject to it from others regardless of the sphere in which we operate, whether that's as a stay-at-home mum, a politician, an athlete or a teacher. If your life interfaces with others in

You are only able to lead people to the degree to which your influence with them is developed.

any way, then you are an influencer. Like power, influence is 'value-neutral' and is subjective in that it depends on the parties within the relationship. It can be positive or it can be negative. You are only able to lead people to the degree to which your influence with them is developed.

RELATIONAL CAPITAL
The business term 'relational capital' is often used to describe the core of the relationship between businesses and their customers. In leadership, it defines the relational wealth that is continually created between people. Relational capital is necessary in order for people to follow a leader. Wise leaders invest in relational capital.

Recently, whilst discussing this term with a relative who works in a Wall Street investment bank, she commented that she and her colleagues apply a similar concept when dealing with their clients. She explained that they invest in the client relationship to the point where the client feels 'indebted' and desires to return the favour. In most other organisations, this would be categorised as corporate hospitality. Businesses understand the need to invest in relationships and, so, it is often the case that a significant portion of the organisation's budget is allocated to this end.

While relational capital in leadership starts out in a similar way, it's not coercive. The aim of the investment (in the relationship) is not to simply reap a reward in the future; building up the individuals involved is also an objective. Investing in relationships leads to a caring and trusting association that is strong enough to cause a person to willingly work with the leader, rather than from a feeling of indebtedness.

Building relational capital is simple but costly, not in monetary terms, but in self-sacrifice for the benefit of others. It is cultivated when we listen to the issues and concerns of others and seek to help where possible, or by investing our time and other resources in people, demonstrating our belief in people and encouraging them, and becoming a more useful resource to people. When we do these things, we are making deposits into a relational account that eventually yields high dividends in influence.

This was the principle that David, the appointed King of Israel, used when raising an army of followers, most of whom started out as societal rejects. He raised and invested in these men to the point where they were willing to risk their lives for him:

'During harvest time, three of the thirty chief warriors came down to David at the cave of Adullam, while a band of Philistines was encamped in the Valley of Rephaim. At that time David was in the stronghold, and the Philistine garrison was at Bethlehem. David longed for water and said, "Oh, that someone would get me a drink of water from the well near the gate of Bethlehem!" So the three mighty warriors broke through the Philistine lines, drew water from the well near the gate of Bethlehem and carried it back to David. But he refused to drink it; instead, he poured it out before the LORD. "Far be it from me, LORD, to do this!" he said. "Is it not the blood of men who went at the risk of their lives?" And David would not drink it. Such were the exploits of the three mighty warriors.' – 2 Samuel 23:13-17 (NIV)

Mike Bonem and Roger Patterson in their book, *Leading from the Second Chair*, suggested that long-term, successful leadership within organisations is based on influence developed through strong relationships and wise decisions.[1] Building influence is essential to building and sustaining leadership. Building influence is harder for subordinates than it is for the boss; nevertheless, it can still be achieved. The following principles could aid that process.

BUILDING INFLUENCE – THE 5 I's OF INFLUENCE

Influence is a very interesting thing. Over the years, I have studied the lives of notable leaders to understand how they became, and continue to be, influential. I have also observed those who have had the greatest influence upon my life. While no two leaders are the same and consequently, exert their influence in different ways I have observed 5 tendencies that are common to people who wield a lot of influence. These people tend to:

1. Act with Integrity
2. Invest their resources in people
3. Interact regularly with the people they influence
4. Intercede on behalf of those they influence
5. Incarnate

Acting with Integrity

The UK parliamentary expenses scandal, which rocked Westminster, from the cabinet to backbenchers and across party lines, called into question the integrity of many of those elected to public office for the purpose of leading the nation. A practice of exploiting the system of parliamentary allowances to subsidise their lifestyles led to the imprisonment of four members of Parliament and two members of the House of Lords. A few others are still being investigated. At the root of this expense scandal is a lack of integrity. As a result of the scandal, the credibility of many politicians was lost and so was their influence with the electorate within their constituencies. With such public and high-profile lapses, it was not a surprise that some politicians lost their bids for re-election.

Integrity is a leader's best friend. To lose integrity is to lose face and initiate a fall from grace.

Integrity is a leader's best friend. To lose integrity is to lose face and initiate a fall from grace.

In chapter 4, I discussed the need for a leader to be a person of integrity. It's worth emphasizing that integrity is crucial when it comes to having real influence. Integrity is required, not just in the big things, but even more so in the small and seemingly insignificant things. In fact, integrity is maintained by taking care of the little things such as avoiding telling little white lies.

Jesus was referring to His life of integrity in John 14:30 when he said '...the ruler of this world is coming, and he has nothing in Me.' He lived His life in such a way that when His enemies sought to justify His execution, they had to obtain false testimonies in order to find Him guilty of anything. This is the standard that God expects leaders to aspire to – to be blameless.

Integrity commits itself to character over personal gain, to people over things, to service over power, to principles over convenience, to the long view over the immediate.[2] It is the foundation upon which many other qualities, such as trustworthiness and respectfulness, are built. Across all levels in any organisation, having integrity is always a prized virtue.

Honesty and transparency go a long way in building integrity into any relationship. Integrity itself begins with conscious decisions, which are better made in advance of a situation. It is a choice to live by a strict moral code, which is above reproach. Personally, my integrity is one thing I work hard to keep intact.

Investing their resources in people

A lot of people have invested in my life, including my family, friends, work colleagues, bosses, academic tutors to name a few. The most prized investment in my life has been in the time spent with key people in my life. These moments have afforded me the opportunity to ask questions, envision the future, and share new ideas and information gleaned from books, CDs, workshops and seminars. I have realised that the greatest investments are not necessarily material in nature, but those aimed at transforming the individual's mindset in a way that causes them to aspire to greater dreams and goals that can benefit the lives of many others. The people who have the greatest influence on me personally are those who have invested in my life in this way. As you invest in people, you also build your stock of influence with them.

At first, it was very difficult for me to get my head around the need to invest in people. I guess, perhaps, looking back now, I would say it was because I grew up being quite self-centred in my outlook. The only time I ever thought about others were times when I could see a benefit for myself.

While it is true that with investments you expect a return, in this case, the return is the other individual's growth and independence. Interestingly, in addition to developing people, investing in people has the incidental results of fostering loyalty and obedience. Investing in people should be borne out of a genuine care and concern for others. These investments can be made through suggesting aids for personal development of the spirit, soul and body, spending time together, offering words of encouragement, and many other ways that have a great and lasting impact.

Interestingly, in addition to developing people, investing in people has the incidental results of fostering loyalty and obedience.

Parents gain influence with their children as they spend time with them, provide for them, create opportunities for fun and laughter, encourage and guide them, and take part in other activities that add value to their children. Similarly, positive influencers seek to add value. I read a story about a disabled man who had just acquired a dog which had been trained to help him with little errands around the house. On receipt of the trained guide dog, the man was told that in order to ensure that the dog continued to respond to him, he should feed the dog himself and not delegate this task to anyone else. Doing so would ensure that the dog developed a relationship with its owner and also see the owner as his master. Though human beings are not the same as dogs, there is a principle worth noting here. Any relationship you invest in consistently will surely deepen the bond between the parties in such a way that allows one to influence the other positively.

For most of us, it is not what we are, but what we think we're not that holds us back. By encouraging people, we can bolster their faith in themselves and elevate their aspirations. Ralph Waldo Emerson said, 'Trust men and they will be true to you, treat them greatly and they will show themselves great.' Words of encouragement could transform a person's life forever.

For most of us, it is not what we are, but what we think we're not that holds us back.

Interact regularly with the people they influence

Leadership is relational. Whether we know it or not, every interaction we have with people either increases or diminishes our influence with them. Good leaders know this and they are always working on improving in this area. For some people, interacting with people is easy whilst for others, it is hard work. However, it is essential for anyone seeking to gain considerable influence with others.

When people walk away after having interacted with you, do they feel better or worse about themselves? Most times in our interactions with others, we want them to think more highly of us, whereas interactions that lead to influence get people to think more highly of themselves. Queen Victoria once remarked, 'After speaking with Gladstone, I felt he was one of the cleverest people in England, but after speaking with Disraeli, I felt I was one of the cleverest women in England.' Gladstone and Disraeli were two highly influential leaders, yet they had very different impacts on those they interacted with. Disraeli appears to have learnt to listen and to understand people better than Gladstone. Little wonder that Disraeli had a better relationship with the Queen!

In our daily interactions, approximately 9 percent of our time is spent writing, 16 percent is spent reading, 30 percent is spent speaking and the remaining 45 percent of the day is spent listening. [3] These percentages show the degree of their importance in our interactions. Thus, development **every interaction we have with people either increases or diminishes our influence with them.** in these four activities in the same order will greatly enhance our influence. In the chapter on the competencies of a leader, we already considered communication as a key competency. Effective communication is not talking, it is listening. [4] David Schwartz's thoughts on the topic in his book, *The Magic of Thinking Big* reflect my own. He said, 'Big people monopolise the listening. Small people monopolise the talking.' It is much easier to talk than to listen, and even much more difficult to listen attentively. Active listening requires full attention, which is a skill most people do not possess.

I have in the past been accused of not being attentive during conversations with others as I had the habit of occasionally glancing around me or attempting to do other things while people were speaking to me. This often gave the impression that I was uninterested in the conversation, which was often not the case. It is a bad habit that I formed while growing up. I have since learnt that by not giving people my full attention during a conversation I was inadvertently giving people the wrong impression: rudeness or a lack of interest in what others have to say. When this happens, people don't feel that they have been listened to and are unlikely to seek your opinion in future matters of importance to them.

In our interactions with others, it is true that when we do most of the talking, we are not really learning much from the other person. This is why leaders in organisations need to take time out to listen to their subordinates. Sam Walton understood this very well. On one occasion, he was said to have asked his pilot to meet him in the next city, whilst he himself travelled several hundred miles with one of the Wal-Mart truck drivers in order to listen and understand things from a Wal-Mart driver's perspective.

Intercede on behalf of those they influence

The Latin root of the word intercede means, 'to act or interpose on behalf of someone in difficulty or challenge.' The story of David recorded in 1 Samuel 17:34-35 illustrates what it means to intercede.

'But David said to Saul, "Your servant used to keep his father's sheep, and when a lion or a bear came and took a lamb out of the flock, I went out after it and struck it, and delivered the lamb from its mouth; and when it arose against me, I caught it by its beard, and struck and killed it.'

To intercede is to intervene in the problems and issues that impact other people. Problems and challenges are commonplace in life and people that come alongside others and help to resolve such issues gain influence with the people they help. Interceding means standing on the side of justice for the disadvantaged and helping them fight their battles.

Those who have influenced me the most have been those people whose efforts have either directly or indirectly helped me to navigate particularly challenging phases of my life. Such help has taken many different forms. Often times, when we think of interceding or standing up for others, we may think of people such as Martin Luther King Jr., who greatly influenced many people because of his stance on rights and equality for people of colour in America. Or perhaps we might think of a company CEO whose efforts helped save several thousand jobs. However, it's important to remember that besides these great acts of intercession, on a daily basis all around us in our workplaces, churches and communities people are engaging in heroic acts of kindness that alleviate the burdens or concerns of others. The housewife who mobilises people on her street into Neighbourhood Watch teams to ensure that homes are kept safe while her neighbours are at work or the teenager who speaks up for a classmate suffering from persistent bullying are examples of intercessors too. When we act in this way towards others, we increase our influence with them.

In the spiritual sense, to intercede is to "stand in the gap" in the place of prayer for others in order to help them gain victory in their challenges. In his book *Prayer Evangelism*,[5] Ed Silvoso said that when we pray for the well-being of the people around us, they begin to open up to us. He further implied that people are able to 'feel' the prayers of others. I had a personal experience of this when a lady from my church told me that she knew that I was praying for her. My wife and I had been praying for her regularly and had not discussed it with the lady in question. She had discerned it. When we genuinely pray for people, we build a spiritual connection, which strengthens the relationship and thus creates room for influencing.

Incarnate or embodying the principles one claims to believe in

The Bible states in John 1:14, 'And the word became flesh and dwelt amongst us, and we beheld His glory, the glory as of the only begotten of the Father, full of grace and truth.' God demonstrated that it was insufficient for Jesus to remain in Heaven giving us instructions to live by. In order for Him to fully influence us, He became like us and modelled for us the life that God wanted us to live. Christ did not only come to die for our sins; He also came to show us how to live. Jesus became the message.

The word incarnate means to embody in flesh, to become something in a tangible form. When I think of Jesus, I think of love. He came with a message of love for all humanity and died for the same cause. When I think of the late Mother Theresa, I think of servanthood, as one who spent the better part of her life serving and meeting the needs of the poorest of the poor in India. When I think of Pastor E. A. Adeboye, the general overseer of the RCCG movement, holiness comes to mind. That is, holiness is the ethos of Pastor Adeboye's ministry and even those of other religious persuasions find it difficult to fault his conduct and life. The late Gandhi said, 'You must be the change you want to see in the world.' He understood this as he sought to engender a generation of protesters in India who were capable of participating in non-violent protest. It was Gandhi's approach of peaceful, civil disobedience in India that greatly influenced Martin Luther King's non-violent approach to political protest.

Leaders who have exerted great influence first became the change they sought to see. The best leaders know that they must change before they can expect to see the desired change in others. It is always easier to instruct and challenge others to live up to certain values than it is to personally imbibe those values one's self. Before making demands that others demonstrate good time-keeping, I had to learn to first work on my own time keeping. Punctuality had to become an integral part of my daily lifestyle not just when I had meetings or appointments, but in everything that I did. Once I made that change, those around came to realise the value I place on time, and now, are increasingly being influenced by that. No amount of words can effect such a change in others unless it is first exemplified by the person seeking to effect the change.

In the letter to Corinth, the apostle Paul asked the Corinthians to 'imitate him' or be influenced by him, even as he was being influenced by Christ (1 Corinthians 11:1). He was merely saying that they should allow themselves to be influenced by him to the degree that he (Paul) embodied the message of Christ.

Thinking which is based on the maxim, 'Do as I say, not as I do' creates a warped concept of leadership and often leads to bad influence. Leaders don't just talk the talk; they lead others in walking the

> **Leaders don't just talk the talk; they lead others in walking the walk.**

walk. Albert Schweitzer, the late German theologian, once said, 'Being an example is not the main thing in influencing others; it is the only thing.'

Influence is evident in people's readiness to follow you and their desire to include you in key decisions and initiatives. [6] Anyone at any level within an organisation can gain influence by practicing the 5 I's of Influence outlined above. Jesus practiced them and His influence is still being felt the world over, even today.

CHAPTER SEVEN

BALANCING THE PARADOX OF THE LEADING FOLLOWER

'And He sat down, called the twelve, and said to them, "If anyone desires to be first, he shall be last of all and servant of all."' – Mark 9:35

'It needs more skill than I can tell to play the second fiddle well.' – C. H. Spurgeon

I have listened to dozens of messages based on biblical teachings of the story of Joseph. His life journey lends itself to a myriad of lessons, some of which have been taught in this book already. However, in this chapter we shall be exploring his role as a subordinate leader. Joseph's rise to fame is very intriguing. He started out with a very proud and arrogant heart but finished as a humble man. He never owned much, but he ended up being put in charge of everything. A journey of 12 years took him from the pit through the prison system and finally, settled in the palace where he ended up ruling over all of Egypt, second only in authority to Pharaoh. In that 12-year period, his 'resume', as recorded in Genesis 39, showed that Joseph had oversight of Potiphar's house and while in prison, the prison warden also gave him oversight over all the other prisoners.

When we contrast Joseph's dreams in Genesis 37, in which he saw all his family members including his father, Jacob, bowing down to him, with what became of him in Potiphar's house, his experiences of prison and in Pharaoh's palace, we noted several things. Firstly, we see that not only did he eventually become a leader, with many bowing down to serve him, but also that God ensured that he always had one person of greater authority to whom he had to bow. On this journey, Joseph, the one who dreamt of leading everyone also learnt to follow. The lesson of Joseph as a leading follower or subordinate leader is paradoxical. He was wired to lead, dreamt of leading, became a leader, yet served in subordinate roles. His story reads like that of many subordinate leaders and it is one with which I am familiar. For many, this well-worn path could be frustrating and even seem unproductive.

Though Joseph evidently had the gift of interpreting dreams and very excellent leadership skills, he remained in a subordinate role to those who were, perhaps less gifted than he was in those areas.

Bonem and Patterson[1] described three main paradoxes that best describes the contradictions inherent in the role of the subordinate leader. They are:

1. The subordinate-leader paradox: This refers to the need of the subordinate leader to have the boldness to initiate and take responsibility, while faithfully submitting to the authority of the lead leader

2. The deep-wide paradox: This describes the need for a subordinate leader to have a broad knowledge of everything within the remit of the work, yet maintaining the ability to keep an eye on the detail to a sufficient degree

3. Contentment-dreaming paradox: This term describes the ability to envision or imagine innovative and creative ways of delivering organisational goals within the constraints of the organisation's vision without losing sight of the wider world or the future

The suggestion is that subordinate leaders are most effective when they are able to function within the tension of the paradoxes explained above by focusing on three aspects of the subordinate's life, namely:

- Relationships, which helps balance the subordinate-leader paradox
- Work habits, which if gotten right can help balance the deep-wide paradox, and
- Emotions for the contentment-dreaming paradox.

Another interesting part of Joseph's story is the fact that Joseph, the ambitious young man from Israel managed to remain content while serving in a subordinate capacity. In fact he managed to do this effectively for the rest of his life. Joseph played a pivotal role in shaping the nation of Egypt despite the fact that he never became the main leader i.e.

Pharaoh. This reinforces a point I made earlier in this book, the magnitude of the impact we have as leaders is not dependent on the positions we occupy but on the influence we exert and the extent to which we transform lives and situations. For some of us, a subordinate position is merely a stopgap to a lead leadership role, while for others, it is the height of their life's achievement. The reality is that not all subordinates will become the main or lead leaders. That being the case, in order to be most effective in what God has entrusted to each one, it is necessary to know how to lead within the tensions of a subordinate leader role.

Being effective as a subordinate leader means being able to get others to cooperate with you and willing to overcome a lot of resistance with limited or no formal authority. It requires the ability and willingness to 'manage' your boss effectively. Finally, it also means being able and willing to cope not just with individuals, but with human systems too – systems comprising the many built-in interrelationships. [2]

The seeming contradictions identified by Bonem and Patterson and explained above are an ever-present reality for many subordinate leaders. In fact they are just a few of the challenges that need to be overcome by many subordinate leaders in order to find fulfilment in the subordinate role regardless of whether it's their final 'destination' or on the way to their destined leading role. Let's explore some of these other challenges and tensions:

DECISION MAKING

To what extent can you make decisions and judgement as a leader without crossing the line of your designated authority? This is a question every subordinate leader grapples with. This is not a trivial matter as your boss' leadership style is a complicating factor. Some bosses are hands-on and really like to be involved with every decision, whilst others give subordinates free reign to make key decisions and only expect the subordinate to involve them when major problems arise or at points of significant change. Another factor that plays a key role in the degree of decision-making freedom you have is the relationship and the level of trust that has been built (influence) with your boss. In my own case, my boss generally gives me free reign in this area. This is down to the deep, trusting relationship we have developed over many years. I have learnt that when apprising him of unfamiliar and difficult situations for which I require his input for decision-making he prefers that I prepare two to three options, along with their related pros and cons, we then discuss each option in detail before reaching a final decision.

This activity enables me to further understand his thought process. As a result I'm better able to deal with similar issues on my own in the future. This approach also satisfies my desire to participate in crucial decision making. . This smooth operating process contradicts the challenges, in the area of decision-making that I faced when I initially took on the role. Back then, my hands-on or 'let's work through an option' approach contrasted with my boss' more cerebral, deliberative approach to decision-making. For a long time, I was frustrated as I felt that I was going about things the wrong way. However, I'm pleased to say that with patient observation and constant evaluation, I eventually came to understand my boss' decision-making style and managed to adapt my processes in order to better align with his.

This clash of decision-making styles and the consequent need for adjustments should be expected because all leaders (whether they are main leaders or subordinate ones) are 'wired' in a way that causes them to want to take responsibility. However in the end the main leader has the final say when it comes to decision-making and so the subordinate leader has to learn to understand his or her boss' modus operandi in this crucial area. In the same way, being clear with your team on their level of responsibility and how you want information (needed for decision-making) to be presented to you will engender a seamless working relationship.

REPRESENTATION
It is in the nature of leadership for those with leadership tendencies to want to create their own identities. The tension here, however, is that for as long as you're in a subordinate role, you need to be mindful of the fact that when you're representing your boss externally you must do so in keeping with the organisational culture, however that is defined by the main leader. A departure from the culture of the organisation could be interpreted as disloyalty or rebellion.

> **It is in the nature of leadership for those with leadership tendencies to want to create their own identities.**

When Ed Milliband was elected as the leader of the UK Labour Party in 2011, one of the first things he sought to do was to distance himself from the shadows of former Prime Ministers Tony Blair and Gordon Brown. In his acceptance speech as the Labour leader, he alluded to being his own man, with his own message and vision for the party. He could only legitimately do this once he became the party leader and not whilst he was a minister in the governments led by either of the two previous leaders. Every subordinate leader needs to understand that while under the leadership of another, the message you consistently present to all the stakeholders must align with that of the main leader. It is only normal to hold some differing views, but whilst under the leadership of another and acting under the office of another, the message has to be consistent with that proclaimed by the main or senior leader. The renowned military leader, General Powell once commented that while he encourages his subordinates to disagree with him in private if necessary, once a decision has been reached, each person has to own it and speak of it as theirs.

Each organisation has its own unique way of working. For example, Bill Hewlett and David Packard, who founded HP, developed a unique style of management that came to be known as *The HP Way*. In Hewlett's words, the *HP Way* was 'a core ideology...which includes a deep respect for the individual, a dedication to affordable quality and reliability, a commitment to community responsibility, and a view that the company exists to make technical contributions for the advancement and welfare of humanity.' [3] Each staff member of HP is duty-bound to portray this ideology in negotiations with external stakeholders.

VISION

When it comes to matters of leadership, vision is critical. That is because leaders lead based on the vision of the future they see. The role of the subordinate leader is to amplify this vision, to execute it, and give it legs to stand on. However, when a subordinate leader has a different vision to that of the boss or main leader, it always leads to 'di-vision' or 'double vision'. 'Double vision' occurs when there are two (di) or more visions in an organisation. It may be acceptable that a subordinate might hold different views on minor elements of the vision, but when it comes to the execution of

Double vision' occurs when there are two (di) or more visions in an organisation.

the overarching vision for the organisation, it has to be implemented in accordance with what has been agreed with the leader. Many church splits and divisions within other organisations, have been attributed to a failure to resolve 'double vision'. When there is major divergence between the subordinate's opinion on the organisational vision and that of the main leader, the most honourable thing to do is tender your resignation. The vision issue is unlikely to go away, and like a vehicle headed for a destination that differs from yours, once you ascertain that the vision is not one you want to go along with, it is best to get off rather than staying on board and causing an unnecessary commotion for others who are keen to go along with the vision.

I often have people share with me their vision for the organisation they work for, and in some cases, I wonder why they have not left the organisation and started one of their own. If they believe so strongly in their own vision, then they are doing themselves (and the organisations they currently work in) a disservice by continuing to subject themselves to a vision they oppose.

TIME MANAGEMENT
When we go to work, we give our time in exchange for alternative resources which we consider to be beneficial to us, such as money. In a sense your time ceases to be yours, as someone else determines what you do with it.

This is one of the biggest tensions faced by the subordinate leader – the fact that most of the time your priorities are shaped by those of your boss, and that they change depending on what the boss decides is a priority. The reality is that this will remain the case.

The deep-wide paradox mentioned earlier in this chapter describes how sub-tier leaders have wide responsibilities and yet are expected to also have a detailed knowledge of each of their areas of responsibility. These demands on the subordinate leader warrant making time management a priority. Lack of proper time management skills could cause burnout and varied illnesses associated with mental strain, which ultimately lead to a loss of valuable working time. The effect extends beyond the sphere of work and often impacts one's private/family life.

Prioritizing, scheduling, delegation and the ability to courteously say no are some time management tips that help ensure effective working practices. Prioritizing is about knowing the things that are important and acting on them in the order of their importance (in the event that you are not sure what is more important, ask your boss). Scheduling has to do with ordering one's work in a way that ensures that blocks of your time are allocated to work that needs doing, in the order of their priority. Any unallocated time leaves room for unimportant activities to encroach upon one's agenda. Delegating is the act of assigning a task, and the commensurate authority to act on the task, to a

Any unallocated time leaves room for unimportant activities to encroach upon one's agenda.

subordinate. To delegate is not to abdicate responsibility, so it requires you to regularly monitor your team-member's progress. Finally, learning to courteously say no is a very important time management skill. You don't have to and, nor should you take on every assignment going. Nor should you aim to attend every meeting. Identifying what is important and courteously rejecting other activities is a very helpful activity.

LOYALTY

Loyalty is an essential component of a healthy boss/subordinate relationship. Loyalty is synonymous with allegiance. It is the act of being faithful to one's commitments, which in this context includes one's boss and subordinates. This isn't a small matter as it is far easier to shift allegiance than to remain loyal to another mortal being. Recently, I learnt a very important lesson from a friend who works as a personal assistant to a British member of Parliament. In the course of our conversation, he mentioned that his boss was gay. Though as a Christian my friend's values are at odds with this lifestyle choice, I was really impressed with his admiration and respect for his boss. He was not blind to the latter's faults, but having decided to serve, he chose to serve him wholeheartedly, and this I found laudable. The lesson for me is that while I might not always agree with all of my boss' choices, I can still remain loyal to him.

Being loyal to your boss or subordinates often means that you have to be identified with their position. Bob Sorge said that, 'Loyalty is that quality that determines with whom you will stand when everyone at the scene must choose a side.' [4] This does not, however, mean that you compromise your moral position, nor does it mean that you have to agree with them at all times; it just means that you remain true to yourself and also seek to protect the integrity of the relationship. Loyalty is displayed by a tame tongue in public and a practice of dealing with any disagreements that may arise, in private. [5]

Being loyal to your boss or subordinates often means that you have to be identified with their position.

Loyalty is a rare quality, and it is easier to be disloyal than to remain loyal to a boss. All it takes for disloyalty to begin to fester are relatively minor things such as entertaining malicious gossip or to allow disagreements to go unresolved. Several years ago, a member of our church, who also happened to be a dear friend took offence with my pastor. When I learnt of it, because I knew that her grievance was unfounded, I purposed in my heart not to welcome or give her any opportunity to infect me with her bitterness, though we were close.

We live in a world where people casually transfer their loyalty from one person to another or from one group to another. Whilst there is nothing wrong with shifting allegiances when one's beliefs or views change, the problem is often caused by the manner in which we do it. Let's be clear, shifting allegiance is often a treacherous path, but should not warrant disloyalty or betrayal. If you choose to shift your loyalty, you should try to keep your integrity with regards to your previous allegiances.

TACT AND DIPLOMACY

Many people do not enjoy healthy relationships with others because they lack tact and diplomacy. Tensions arise, relationships disintegrate, walls go up, and barriers are built, all because careful consideration is not paid to what is being said and *how* it is being said. To be tactful requires one to have a keen sense of what to say or do to avoid causing offence unnecessarily. When interacting with others, it is an inevitable fact that there will be differences of opinion and understanding. As such, it is necessary to be tactful in order to ensure the relationships are maintained.

Many brilliant ideas are rejected each and every day because of a lack of tact and diplomacy by those who present them. A while ago, I went for a meeting attended by community leaders within my city and one of the speakers at the meeting spoke passionately on his views and I must admit that much of what he said made sense. He went on to say that he advises top city officials in London on issues that relate to young people in London, but then said that they never accept his advice. At first this puzzled me, but as I continued to listen to him speak, the reasons why they might shun his advice soon became apparent. Though he spoke with a strong passion and made very meaningful contributions, he lacked tact in conveying his views. I remember thinking to myself that with such an attitude, if I were one of these city officials, I would probably struggle to accept his counsel too.

> **Many brilliant ideas are rejected each and every day because of a lack of tact and diplomacy by those who present them.**

Proverbs 14:3 (NLT) says, 'A fool's proud talk becomes a rod that beats him, but the words of the wise keep them safe.' The best subordinate leaders are not driven by the ambition to get ahead of others, but by the desire to get along with people irrespective of who they are within the organisation. Consequently, they mind their words and actions with others and carefully seek their buy-in.

SUBMISSION AND AUTHORITY

As has been mentioned elsewhere in this book, authority is usually positional and this type of authority is often the trump card played by leaders who lack any real influence with their subordinates. The most effective leaders lead through their influence. Having said that, authority is nonetheless essential. The complex web of human relations needs it in order to function optimally. It was Satan's (Lucifer) rebellion against God's authority that led to his downfall.

'How you are fallen from heaven, O Lucifer, son of the morning! How you are cut down to the ground, You who weakened the nations! For you have said in your heart: "I will ascend into heaven, I will exalt my throne above the stars of God; I will also sit on the mount of the congregation On the farthest sides of the north"' – Isaiah 14:12-13

Some time ago, I was called upon by one of the heads of department that reports to me to intervene in a long-standing issue he was having with one of his team members. The head of department had an extremely talented team member that refused to serve under his leadership. I had raised this matter with the individual on a few previous occasions, but he continued to struggle with submission and eventually left the team. This was in spite of the fact that he felt quite stimulated by working in that area. He resigned his place in the department and now sits on the sidelines, all because he was not willing to serve under a delegated authority.

The head of department was acting on the authority I had delegated to him, authority which had been similarly delegated to me and which could ultimately be traced back to God. Sadly, the team member failed to see beyond the head of the department. An attitude of submission is not a loss of authority. It is recognition of the source of authority.[6] This is what the individual in the example above failed to realise. All authority is transferred or delegated, and having this understanding helps the subordinate leader to relate to the different levels of authority that exist around him or her. It also helps for the subordinate leader to come to accept that as a leader in the middle of the organisation, he or she is unlikely to ever have the final say, nor the ultimate responsibility for any action or decision. Having such an attitude helps to keep all the relationships in proper perspective.

The notable composer and conductor Leonard Bernstein was asked which instrument he considered to be the most difficult to play. After a short pause, he said, 'second fiddle.' He explained further by saying, 'I can get plenty of first violinists, but to find one who can play second fiddle with enthusiasm – that's a problem.' In an orchestra, the second fiddle refers to the secondary or supporting violin. Like the second fiddle, the subordinate leader always plays a secondary role and this, likewise, is a difficult role to play, but I hope that with the points discussed in this chapter, it is a role that you will feel better able to play with genuine enthusiasm.

CHAPTER EIGHT

DR SOLA FOLA-ALADE: HOW TO INFLUENCE YOUR BOSS

'Also Daniel petitioned the king, and he set Shadrach, Meshach, and Abed-Nego over the affairs of the province of Babylon.' – Daniel 2:49

'Leadership is the art of getting someone else to do something you want done — because he wants to do it.' – General Dwight Eisenhower

Over the last two decades or so, the teaching and theme of leadership has become quite commonplace both in the secular and spiritual world alike.

Almost every bookshop or library has a leadership section, but in my entire study life, I have hardly seen a book on effective followership. I guess that is because such a book would hardly appeal to the senses of the masses. One man put it this way, 'If we all become leaders who will be the followers.'

I presume the more appropriate way to look at it is that no one is really ever born into a leadership position; every great leader was first an 'effective follower'.

A wise man said, 'The only job where you start at the top is grave digging.' I suppose he meant, if you don't want to end up digging the grave of your career, start at the bottom like everybody else. In fact, like the theme of this book implies, cultivate and maintain a 'servant's heart' even when you get to the top of the organisation.

Every great leader first served or understudied other leaders before they assumed or served in a leadership position. Like a crown prince, they might have been born with the right or privilege to lead, but still have to be prepared before assuming their leadership position. Even Prince William, the future King of England, only just became a colonel in the British Army and has had to report to and refer to many generals in the same army as 'boss' before he eventually becomes the King of England.

Of course, if it is agreed that no one really starts their leadership journey from the top, the question then is how can we influence our boss on our way there?

DANIEL IN BABYLON

Daniel is one of my favourite characters in the Bible simply because he exemplified both the practical and the prophetic dimensions of leadership. Like Joseph, he wielded great influence in his dealings with the kings and leaders of his time.

During the reign of Nebuchadnezzar, king of Babylon, Daniel and his three other friends were headhunted from Judah to come and serve the king in Babylon.

'Then the king ordered Ashpenaz, chief of his court officials, to bring into the king's service some of the Israelites from the royal family and the nobility— young men without any physical defect, handsome, showing aptitude for every kind of learning, well informed, quick to understand, and qualified to serve in the king's palace.'
– Daniel 1:3-4

Amongst those chosen, Daniel and his three friends were outstanding in all matters of wisdom and excellence and as a result were called to serve before the king. Before long, Daniel established himself as the go to person in the kingdom, because of his ability to solve problems and his unflinching character.

Though Daniel was in Babylonian captivity, he managed to rise and become a key influencer in Babylon. According to the Bible, his influence spanned the reign of three kings of Babylon:

- Daniel made the king acknowledge his God: 'The king answered Daniel, and said, "Truly your God *is* the God of gods, the Lord of kings, and a revealer of secrets, since you could reveal this secret."' – Daniel 2:47

- He was rewarded by the king: 'Then the king promoted Daniel and gave him many great gifts; and he made him ruler over the whole province of Babylon, and chief administrator over all the wise men of Babylon.' – Daniel 2:48
- He influenced the king, to appoint his colleagues as administrators: 'Also Daniel petitioned the king, and he set Shadrach, Meshach, and Abed-Nego over the affairs of the province of Babylon.' – Daniel 2:49
- He made King Darius recognise the power of his God: 'I make a decree that in every dominion of my kingdom men must tremble and fear before the God of Daniel.' – Daniel 6:26

WHAT DOES YOUR BOSS WANT?

General Dwight Eisenhower's definition of leadership most accurately describes the best way to lead your boss. He says, 'Leadership is the art of getting someone else to do something you want done — because he wants to do it.'

A first step then in effectively influencing another person (your boss) in a particular direction is to first find out what he/she wants.

HELP YOUR BOSS SUCCEED IN ALL THAT HE DOES

After almost two and a half decades of leading and serving other leaders, my conclusion is that the best way to influence your boss (or anyone) is to help him/her succeed in every area of their life. If you can genuinely make your boss's working life easier and more productive, his/her vision a reality, his/her personal and family life more peaceful and enjoyable, you become an invaluable asset to him/her and hence will have his/her ears, attention and heart.

NINE WAYS YOU CAN BECOME AN ASSET TO YOUR BOSS
1. Solutions

People always appreciate a person who helps solve their problems. In fact, we tend to gravitate towards people who are problem solvers and we avoid those who cause or increase our problems. Every boss appreciates an employee or direct report who is a problem solver in his department or organisation.

The first place to start solving problems is on the job you are paid to do. Employers do not hire or pay people to fill positions, hold a title, or sit at a desk. Employees are hired to solve a particular problem for the organisation; for example, a sales manager is hired to ensure that more clients are brought into the organisation, subsequently increasing the total revenue of the company. A financial manager is hired and paid to ensure that the organisations financial accounts are in proper order, taxes and suppliers are paid on time, and that the company's money is saved and spent judiciously and in a timely manner.

Contrary to what most employees think, they are not paid to show up at 9 a.m. and leave at 5 p.m., to write memos and push files around; all that is just mere activity. They are paid to increase the organisation's productivity by their actions. Any employee who is able to increase the department, organisation or even the boss' productivity will be considered an asset to the boss and the organisation as a whole. Anyone who doesn't will be seen as a liability or impediment to the boss and organisation.

Seek to be a problem solver on your job first by asking your boss to clarify and outline what problems you were hired to solve and then do them promptly and in an excellent manner. Also ask your boss at the beginning of each week or month to clearly specify what result he/she wants you to achieve by the end of that period and seek to deliver on it in a diligent and prompt manner. Problem solvers win the heart of their boss.

2. Management

Bosses also greatly appreciate when their direct reports are great managers of themselves, resources and their work. Every leader and business owner desires to have a person who is faithful, loyal and diligent in managing their affairs and resources.

People appreciate someone who is so good at managing the organisation or department that it requires little or no input from the boss. This will take a great burden off the boss' shoulders and allow him/her to focus on other important things. A faithful manager frees up the boss' time to be more productive, allows him/her to take a break and spend a stress-free time with the family or enables him/her time to think strategically about where the organisation is going.

3. Initiative

Good initiative is a great complement to good management. Bosses appreciate employees who have and take initiative on things without being prompted. They love people who are able to make effective decisions on their own. They value people who do not always bring problems for them to solve but use their initiative to solve the problems and only tell the boss when the challenge has been put to bed.

4. Reliability (Commitment)
Reliability is what you get when you combine commitment with the other qualities listed above. Every boss dreams and desires to have an employee who is committed, such that you can depend on them to get the important things done without having to look over their shoulder.

The reliable staff will become the go to person for the boss – that is, the most indispensible person within the organisation. He/she becomes the person who the boss goes to when he wants a crucial task done. One way to develop a reputation for reliability is to under promise and to always over deliver and never the other way around.

5. Flexibility
Another quality that makes an employee really attractive to an employer is his/her flexibility. This is an attitude that shows a readiness to change one's own plans at short notice to fit in the boss' request. This also entails the ability to make sacrifices in order to achieve the organisation's objectives. A good employee will get to work at 9 a.m. and leave by 5 p.m., but an exceptional one is ready to get in earlier and leave work later until the desired result is achieved.

6. Integrity (Trust)
In addition to the above qualities, integrity is one virtue that when present, will make the employee an outstanding one. The absence of integrity even in the

presence of all the others is an abysmal situation.

No one wants to live or work with a dishonest person regardless of how competent or charismatic they may be, or how productive or profitable they are to the organisation. If they are dishonest, they will eventually hurt the organisation and its reputation. It is often said that, 'A man's competence will take him to the top, but his lack of character will bring him right down.'

7. **Openness**

Openness is different from honesty (integrity) in that honesty has to do with telling the truth when asked, but openness I believe is a higher standard because it entails saying the truth and declaring one's intentions and motivations even without being asked.

Openness has to do with clearly stating your intentions before taking on the role, including why you really want the job, how long you intend to work with the organisation, if you have plans of starting a similar business in the future or if you have any grievances with the boss or the organisation.

These declarations of intention ensure the boss has no erroneous views concerning your length of stay or future plans. It will help avoid a situation where your boss thinks you intend to stay with the firm long term and, therefore, begins to make expensive and intensive investments in you as an individual with the hope of the organisation reaping the dividends on a longer-term scale.

Honesty and, more importantly, openness create a climate of trust between an employee and his/her boss. Wherever there is trust, it gives the relationship a real chance to grow in an environment of security and stability with very little room for suspicion, strife or conflict.

8. Loyalty

Every boss desires some kind of loyalty from their subordinates to the organisation's cause and to himself. Every boss will look suspiciously at people who run their own personal agenda at the expense of the organisation's interest.

Bosses also particularly desire personal loyalty from their employees. Because of the unavoidable politics and prevalent back talk and competitiveness that is present in many organisations, every boss would like to know that their employees 'have their back' – that they will publicly defend them and privately defend their interest and will not stab them in the back.

A competent and loyal employee is like a safe haven to one's employer.

9. Support (Connection)

Lastly, one added quality that helps to make an ideal employee is the ability to connect with their boss outside of the work environment, such as in their areas of interest, hobbies, etc. It is generally thought that those who engage and network with their boss on the golf course, pub or at other social engagements are usually the ones favoured for promotion. I do not suggest that we become insincere boot lickers, but rather that we become more sociable, flexible and interesting as individuals. It also helps if one is able to connect with and support one's boss on an emotional level, as and when appropriate in such occasions where they lose a loved one or are going through a difficult personal, financial or family issue. It helps to show genuine concern and show as much support as possible in these situations.

The development and demonstration of each of the above qualities will ensure that you become and remain an invaluable and indispensable asset to your boss.

When you become an asset, you put your boss in a position and stir up in him/her the disposition to be easily influenced by you and your opinions and guarantee his commitment to ensuring you succeed in every way.

NOTES

Introduction

[1.] John Maxwell, *360-degree Leader: Developing your Influence from Anywhere in the Organisation.* (Tennessee: Thomas Nelson, 2005), page 1.

[2.] Blackaby, Henry & Blackaby, Richard. *Called to be God's Leader: Lessons from the Life of Joshua.* (Tennessee: Thomas Nelson, 2004), page 23.

[3.] John Maxwell, *360-degree Leader: Developing your Influence from Anywhere in the Organisation.* (Tennessee: Thomas Nelson, 2005), page 12.

[4.] Blackaby, Henry & Blackaby, Richard. *Called to be God's Leader: Lessons from the Life of Joshua.* (Tennessee: Thomas Nelson, 2004), page 41.

Chapter One – The Call to Lead

[1.] James Hunter, *The World's Most Powerful Leadership Principle,* (New York: Crown Business, 2004), page 32.

[2.] Blackaby, Henry & Blackaby, Richard. *Spiritual Leadership: Moving People on to God's Agenda*, (Tennessee: B&H Publishing Group, 2001), page 20.

[3.] Blackaby, Henry & Blackaby, Richard. *Spiritual Leadership: Moving People on to God's Agenda*, (Tennessee: B&H Publishing Group, 2001), page 19.

[4.] http://faculty.css.edu/dswenson/web/LEAD/GreatTrait.html

[5] Blackaby, Henry & Blackaby, Richard. *Called to be God's Leader: Lessons from the Life of Joshua,* (Tennessee: Thomas Nelson, 2004), page 39.

[6] Maxwell, John. *21 Irrefutable Laws of Leadership,* (Tennessee: Thomas Nelson, 2007), page 25.

7   http://www.pfdf.org/knowledgecenter/
journal.aspx?ArticleID=840
8   *Adapted from* Barna, George. *Leaders on Leadership:
Wisdom, Advice and Encouragement on the Art of Leading
God's People,* (Copyright, Regal Books, Ventura, CA. Used
with permission, 1997), pages 25-27.

Chapter Two – The Core of Leadership
1   One of the associates of Genistar supplied this
information.
2   Silvoso, Ed. *Anointed for Business: How Christians
Can Use Their Influence in the Marketplace to Change the
World,* (California: Regal Books, 2002), page 183.
3   Ranger O. Terence. *Evangelical Christianity and
Democracy in Africa,* (USA: Oxford University Press,
2008), page 226.
4   http://everything2.com/title/Hansie+Cronje,
15/06/11, 14.14pm
5   Sanders, Oswald. *Spiritual Leadership: Principles
of Excellence for Every Believer.* (Chicago: Moody
Publishers, 2007), page 102.
6   Sanders, Oswald. *Spiritual Leadership: Principles
of Excellence for Every Believer.* (Chicago: Moody
Publishers, 2007), page 107.
7   Peter J. Daniels, *Miss Phillips, You Were Wrong: A
formula to Handle Rejection,* (Published by The House of
Tabor, 1989).
8   Maxwell, John. *360 Degree Leader: Developing your
Influence from Anywhere in the Organisation,* (Tennessee:
Thomas Nelson, 2005), page 220.
9   Southwest Airlines is famously known in the
aviation industry in America as the airline that love built.

Chapter Three – The Character of a Leader

1   Hunter, James. *The World's Most Powerful Leadership Principle: How to become a Servant Leader*, (New York: Crown Business, 2004), page 144.

2   Maxwell, John. *21 Irrefutable Laws of Leadership*, (Tennessee: Thomas Nelson, 2007), page 64.

3   Blackaby, Henry & Blackaby, Richard. *Spiritual Leadership: Moving People on to God's Agenda*, (Tennessee: B&H Publishing Group, 2001), page 104.

4   [Jack Hayford] Barna, George. *Leaders on Leadership: Wisdom, Advice and Encouragement on the Art of Leading God's People*, (California: Regal Books, 1997), page 70.

Chapter Four – Competencies (Skills) of a Leader

1   Sanders, Oswald. *Spiritual Leadership: Principles of Excellence for Every Believer*, (Chicago: Moody Publishers, 2007), page 115.

2   http://butler-bowdon.com/howtowinfriends

3   Quoted in *Everyone Communicates, Few Connect*, John Maxwell (Tennessee: Thomas Nelson, 2010), page 4

4   Barna, George. *Leaders on Leadership: Wisdom, Advice and Encouragement on the Art of Leading God's People*, (California: Regal Books, 1997), page 239.

5   Sanders, Oswald. *Spiritual Leadership: Principles of Excellence for Every Believer*, (Chicago: Moody Publishers, 2007), page 71.

6   Blackaby, Henry & Blackaby, Richard. *Spiritual Leadership: Moving People on to God's Agenda*, (Tennessee: B&H Publishing Group, 2001), page 57.

Chapter Five - Consequences of Leadership

[1] McIntosh, Gary & Rima, Samuel. *Overcoming the Dark Side of Leadership: How to Become an Effective Leader by Confronting Potential Failures*, (Michigan: Baker Books, 2007), page 13.

[2] http://writeablessing.com/airlines.html

[3] Maxwell, John. *21 Irrefutable Laws of Leadership*, (Tennessee: Thomas Nelson, 2007), pages 122-123.

[4] Blackaby, Henry & Blackaby, Richard. *Spiritual Leadership: Moving People on to God's Agenda*, (Tennessee: B&H Publishing Group, 2001), page 265.

[5] Sanders, Oswald. *Spiritual Leadership: Principles of Excellence for Every Believer*, (Chicago: Moody Publishers, 2007), page 156.

[6] McIntosh, Gary & Rima, Samuel. *Overcoming the Dark Side of Leadership: How to Become an Effective Leader by Confronting Potential Failures*, (Michigan: Baker Books, 2007), page 62.

[7] http://www.cipd.co.uk/hr-resources/ factsheets/working-hours-time-off- work.aspx

[8] Blackaby, Henry & Blackaby, Richard. *Spiritual Leadership: Moving People on to God's Agenda*, (Tennessee: B&H Publishing Group, 2001), page 251.

[9] Sorge, Bob. *Dealing with the Rejection and Praise of Man*, (Missouri: Oasis House, 1999), page 42.

Chapter Six – Building Influence

[1] Bonem, Mike & Patterson, Roger. *Leading from the Second Chair: Serving Your Church, Fulfilling Your Role, and Realizing Your Dreams*, (California: Jossey-Bass, 2005), page 12.

[2] Maxwell, John. *Becoming a Person of Influence*, (Tennessee: Thomas Nelson), page 21.

[3] Maxwell, John. *Becoming a Person of Influence*,

(Tennessee: Thomas Nelson), page 90.

[4]   Maxwell, John. *Becoming a Person of Influence*, (Tennessee: Thomas Nelson), page 85.

[5]   Silvoso, Ed. *Prayer Evangelism: How to Change The Spiritual Climate over your Home, Neighbourhood and City*, (California: Regal Books, 2000) pages 42-43.

[6]   Bonem, Mike & Patterson, Roger. *Leading from the Second Chair: Serving Your Church, Fulfilling Your Role, and Realizing Your Dreams*, (California: Jossey-Bass, 2005), page 14.

Chapter Seven – Balancing the Paradox of the Leading Follower

[1]   Bonem, Mike & Patterson, Roger. *Leading from the Second Chair: Serving Your Church, Fulfilling Your Role, and Realizing Your Dreams*, (California: Jossey-Bass, 2005), pages 3-6.

[2]   Kotter P. John, *Power and Influence, Beyond Formal Authority*, (New York: The Free Press, 1985), page 42.

[3]   http://en.wikipedia.org/wiki/Hewlett-Packard

[4]   Sorge, Bob. *Loyalty: The Reach of the Noble Heart*, (Missouri: Oasis House, 2005), page 19.

[5]   Bonem, Mike & Patterson, Roger. *Leading from the Second Chair: Serving Your Church, Fulfilling Your Role, and Realizing Your Dreams*, (California: Jossey-Bass, 2005), page 31.

[6]   Bonem, Mike & Patterson, Roger. *Leading from the Second Chair: Serving Your Church, Fulfilling Your Role, and Realizing Your Dreams*, (California: Jossey-Bass, 2005), page 23.

BIBLIOGRAPHY

Barna, George. Leaders on Leadership: Wisdom, Advice and Encouragement on the Art of Leading God's People. California: Regal Books, 1997.

Blackaby, Henry & Blackaby, Richard. Spiritual Leadership: Moving People on to God's Agenda. Tennessee: B&H Publishing Group, 2001.

Blackaby, Henry & Blackaby, Richard. Called to be God's Leader: Lessons from the Life of Joshua. Tennessee: Thomas Nelson, 2004.

Bonem, Mike & Patterson, Roger. Leading from the Second Chair: Serving Your Church, Fulfilling Your Role, and Realizing Your Dreams. California: Jossey-Bass, 2005.

Cedar, Paul. Strength in Servant Leadership. Texas: Word Books, 1987.

Covey, Stephen. The 7 Habits of Highly Effective People: Powerful Lessons in Personal Change. Sydney: Simon and Schuster, 2004.

Damazio, Frank. The Making of a Leader. Oregon: B T Publishing, 1988.

Fisher, Roger & Sharp, Alan. Getting it Done: How to Lead when you're not in Charge. New York: Harper Collins, 1998.

Hunter, James. The World's Most Powerful Leadership Principle: How to become a Servant Leader. New York:

Crown Business, 2004.

Heward-Mills, Dag. Loyalty and Disloyalty. Ghana: Parchment House, 2003.

Heward-Mills, Dag. The Art of Leadership. Ghana: Parchment House, 2003.

Kotter, John. Power and Influence: Beyond Formal Authority. New York: The Free Press, 1985.

Maxwell, John. 21 Irrefutable Laws of Leadership. Tennessee: Thomas Nelson, 2007.

Maxwell, John. 360 Degree Leader: Developing your Influence from Anywhere in the Organisation. Tennessee: Thomas Nelson, 2005.

Maxwell, John. The Winning Attitude/Developing the Leaders Around You/Becoming a Person of Influence. Tennessee: Thomas Nelson, 2000.

Maxwell. John. Everyone Communicates, Few Connect. Tennessee: Thomas Nelson, 2010.

McIntosh, Gary & Rima, Samuel. Overcoming the Dark Side of Leadership: How to Become an Effective Leader by Confronting Potential Failures. Michigan: Baker Books, 2007.

Osborne, Christina. Leadership. London: Dorling Kindersley (DK) Limited, 2008.

Ranger O. Terence. Evangelical Christianity and Democracy in Africa. USA: Oxford University Press, 2008.

Sanders, Oswald. Spiritual Leadership: Principles of Excellence for Every Believer. Chicago: Moody Publishers, 2007.

Sorge, Bob. Dealing with the Rejection and Praise of Man. Missouri: Oasis House, 1999.

Sorge, Bob. Loyalty: The Reach of the Noble Heart. Missouri: Oasis House, 2005.

Silvoso, Ed. Anointed for Business: How Christians Can Use Their Influence in the Marketplace to Change the World. California: Regal Books, 2002.

Silvoso, Ed. Prayer Evangelism: How to Change The Spiritual Climate over your Home, Neighbourhood and City. California: Regal Books, 2000.

Tracy, Brian. How the Best Leaders Lead: Proven Secrets to Getting the Most Out of Yourself and Others. New York: AMACOM, 2010.

Tracy, Brian. Goals: How to Get Everything you Want Faster than you Ever Thought Possible. California: Berrett-Koehler Publishers, Inc., 2003.

ABOUT THE AUTHOR

Bankole Akinlade currently serves as the Director of Pastoral Care and Outreach within the leadership team of Trinity Chapel, a vibrant Church based in London with a mandate to develop leaders who will influence society. Originally trained as a Business Analyst, Bankole has since  found his place in Christian ministry. He is most passionate about increasing Christian influence within wider society. He recently completed an MA in Theology, Politics and Faith Based Organisations at Kings College London. Bankole loves to read, travel and most of all spend time with his wife and son.